BAY AREA GARDENING

~

Practical Essays by Master Gardeners

~

Edited by
Barbara J. Euser

Copyright 2002 by Marin Master Gardeners
All rights reserved.

For permission to reprint essays in this volume, grateful acknowledgement is made to the holders of copyright named on pages 204-205.

Published by
Writers Center of Marin
1323 Fourth Street
San Rafael, California 94901
Telephone: 415-456-1825
www.writerscenterofmarin.org

Cataloging Data
Bay Area Gardening / edited by Barbara J. Euser
p. cm.
Includes index.
1. Gardening – California. 2. Gardening – Mediterranean climates.
3. Native plants – California. 4. Integrated Pest Management.
5. Master Gardeners.
I. Title. II. Euser, Barbara J.

ISBN: 0-9719666-0-5

Cover and interior illustrations by Maggie Agro
Cover and interior design by Dianne Nelson, Shadow Canyon Graphics

Printed in the United States of America

First Edition
10 9 8 7 6 5 4 3 2 1

Preface

In 1999, the Marin County Master Gardeners began writing a weekly column on a variety of gardening problems for the *Marin Independent Journal*. Very soon their column gained popularity and a devoted readership. People regularly called the University of California Cooperative Extension to gather more information about the issues discussed in the column. It was a very good sign. As readers' interest has grown and developed, so too have the enthusiastic contributions of Master Gardeners, culminating in the publication of *Bay Area Gardening: Practical Essays by Master Gardeners*.

Who are these Master Gardeners? The Master Gardener program was begun by the University of California in 1980 and since then more than 7,000 Master Gardeners have been certified. The training program, conducted by University of California specialists, farm advisors and other experts, may last 15 or more weeks. In return, trained Master Gardeners volunteer their time and expertise to support community gardens, present educational programs and conduct other gardening-related activities.

The Marin County Master Gardener program took root in 1986 and since then has grown to be one of the most effective volunteer horticultural organizations in the Bay area. It reminds me of a garden built from scratch. Every year our Master Gardeners put forth more effort, more work and more volunteer hours. Their assistance to the community increases in size and effectiveness, much like a well-established and beautiful plant.

Bay area residents are very concerned about a maintaining a healthy environment, privacy and gardens as an extension of living spaces. The University of California Cooperative Extension service is overwhelmed with telephone calls and samples to explain and find environmentally friendly solutions for gardening problems. In response to these demands, Master Gardeners in Marin County contributed 10,057 hours of volunteer service in 2001 alone! Master Gardeners in other Bay area counties are similarly active.

Columns written by Marin Master Gardeners are an important part of the overall educational effort of the Master Gardener program. They convey a philosophy of gardening that considers the nature of plants as living things that may blossom and thrive or fall ill in the garden. Readers learn that plants will grow and remain in good health if they are properly cared for, and before attempting to prevent or control a problem, it is essential to identify the nature of the cause. Each essay in this collection clarifies a topic with common sense, practicality, and its applicability for the Bay area's Mediterranean climate.

Bay Area Gardening will help gardeners choose proper remedial action or, in some cases, inaction, in caring for their plants. It offers sound advice on choosing the least toxic method of control of pests and plant diseases. Various plants and types of gardens are explored. What a gold mine of sound advice for gardeners in the Bay area this is, collected in one handy volume.

Pavel Svihra
University of California Horticulture Advisor

Foreword

When I took the Master Gardener course, I was asked on which of the many committees I wished to work. As a writer, the committee that naturally appealed to me was the one that writes weekly educational columns for our local newspaper, the *Marin Independent Journal*. Writing these columns, I began to appreciate the research, care, time and effort Master Gardener writers put into each and every one of them. It seemed a shame that readers had a one-time-only opportunity to read each piece.

A number of people told me they routinely clip the Master Gardener columns and keep them in little stacks. As a person who keeps many such little stacks, I know how difficult it is to find a particular article at the moment I need to refer to it. Publishing a book of Master Gardener articles seemed a good way to alleviate the problem of scattered stacks of cliippings accumulating in houses around the county, as well as to expand the availability of these articles to other gardeners in the Bay area.

Master Gardeners espouse a certain gardening philosophy of reliance on native plants and other climate-appropriate species coupled with integrated pest management using least toxic methods of control that I believe emerges quite clearly from this collection of essays.

As volunteers, Master Gardeners each contribute his or her own set of skills to the organization. The writers represented in this book have each contributed their own personal expertise in writing their articles. The book itself has been very much a team effort. Members of the IJ Commitee volunteered additional time to work on this book. Maggie Agro contributed her artistic talents in creating the illustrations, as well as writing articles and working on the book team. Kathy Reiffenstein, Diane Lynch, Virginia Havel and Lee Oliphant were actively engaged from the initial conceptualization of this book through the final phases of indexing and proofreading. Patricia Bulkley, Maxwell Drever and Michael Weinberger deserve special thanks for their support of this project. The Master Gardeners Board of Directors enthusiastically embraced this new venture, as did the staff at the County Extension office, Ellie Rilla, Director, University of California Cooperative Extension, and Effy Cook.

As Director of the Writers Center of Marin, I was able to offer its assistance to publish the Master Gardener book. The Writers Center of Marin is a non-profit organization dedicated to serving and supporting writers of all genres. Its mission is to serve as a center for the local community of working writers. The Writers Center offers writing workshops and seminars and provides a resource center for members' use.

The Writers Center has developed joint projects with other non-profit organizations including the Bay Area Independent Publishers Association and the Marin Women's Hall of Fame. The Writers Center is an active member of Artworks Downtown, the working center for the arts in San Rafael, and has received grants from the Marin Arts Council for educational programs. It is in the spirit of cooperation and support for other non-profit organizations that the Writers Center is pleased to publish *Bay Area Gardening: Practical Essays by Master Gardeners*.

Barbara J. Euser
Editor

Contents

~

PREFACE iii
FOREWORD v

CHAPTER 1: GARDEN DESIGN AND LANDSCAPING 1
   Perfect Harmony in Your Garden by Julie Carter, Jan Specht,
   Kathy Reiffenstein 2
   Principles of Design by M.C. Dwyer 6
   Think Fire Safe Landscaping by Diane Lynch 9
   Feng Shui in the Garden by Terumi Leinow 12
   Rock Garden Chic by Stacy Nelson 14
   Greenhouses by Maggie Agro 16

CHAPTER 2: CLIMATE AND YOUR GARDEN 19
   Mediterranean Climates and What They Mean to Us
   by Diane Lynch 20
   How Many Climates in Your Garden? by Maggie Agro 23
   Made for the Shade by Maggie Agro 26
   Drought Tolerant Ferns by Barbara J. Euser 29

CHAPTER 3: SOIL, ITS COMPOSITION AND HEALTH 32
   The "Dirt" on Soil by Diane Lynch 33
   Why Should I Mulch? by Julie Carter, Jan Specht,
   Kathy Reiffenstein 36
   Creating Compost—Garden Magic by Diane Lynch 42
   HMO for Healthy Soil by Jan Specht 46
   Diagnosing Common Disorders by Kathy Reiffenstein 50

CHAPTER 4: SEASONAL GARDENING 52
   Plant Some Spring Happiness! by Stacy Nelson 53
   Summer Pruning Slows Overgrown Fruit Trees
   by Diane Lynch 55

November is Time to Plant by Maggie Agro 58
Plant California Native Bulbs This Fall by Barbara J. Euser 60
Preparing the Garden for Winter by Elizabeth Finley 62
Putting Your Garden to Bed by Diane Lynch 64
Winter: To Prune or Not to Prune by Diane Lynch 67

CHAPTER 5: SPECIALIZED GARDENING 71
Tea Gardens by I'Lee Hooker 72
Container Gardening by Kathy Reiffenstein 75
Herbs in Your Own Backyard by I'Lee Hooker 81

CHAPTER 6: HABITAT GARDENING 84
Habitat Gardening by Maggie Agro 85
Butterfly Gardens by Nancy Bauer 87
Where Have All the Songbirds Gone? by Diane Lynch 89
Berries for the Birds by Diane Lynch 92

CHAPTER 7: FLOWERING PLANTS 94
Scented Geraniums, Actually Pelargoniums by Diane Lynch 95
The New Heucheras by I'Lee Hooker 98
Hydrangea Hyperbole by Kathy Reiffenstein 100
Achilleas: Legends and Lore by Barbara J. Euser 103
Not-So-Finicky Fuchsias by I'Lee Hooker 106
Orchids for the Home by Virginia Havel 109
Consider the Lily by Virginia Havel 112

CHAPTER 8: OTHER PLANTS OF SPECIAL INTEREST 114
Landscaping with Ornamental Grasses by Virginia Havel 115
Lawns: Beauty and Beast by Jan Specht 117
Ground Covers by Jan Specht 121
Plants for Clay Soil by Barbara J. Euser 123
Cacti and Succulents by Virginia Havel 129
Landscaping with Ferns by Virginia Havel 129

CHAPTER 9: TREES AND UNDERPLANTINGS 131
Caring for Our Majestic Oaks by Diane Lynch 147
Planting Under Oaks by Barbara J. Euser 135

Sudden Oak Death Update compiled by Diane Lynch
from material by Pavel Svihra, Kim Keirnan, Nicole
Palkovsky, Bruce Hagen, Garey Slaughter,
Andrew Storer, Maggi Kelly 138
The Joy of Japanese Maples by Maggie Agro 141
Native Plants Under Redwoods by Virginia Havel 143

CHAPTER 10: PROPAGATION 146
Divide and Conquer Those Perennials by Diane Lynch 148
Save Seeds for the Tastiest Harvest by Maggie Agro 150
Go Forth and Propagate by Lee Oliphant and Diane Lynch 152

CHAPTER 11: WEEDS AND INVASIVES 155
Exotic Invasives and Misplaced Plants by Diane Lynch 156
A Place for Invasives? by Barbara J. Euser 159

CHAPTER 12: INSECTS, PESTS AND THEIR CONTROL 162
Honey Bees and Their Kin by Virginia Havel 163
Little Miss Muffett and Friends by Jan Specht 166
Scale Insects in the Garden by Jan Specht 169
Spider Mites by Jan Specht 172
Snails, Slugs, and Slime by Jan Specht 174
Ant Control Without Chemicals by Jan Specht 177
Fungus Control for Roses by Jan Specht 180
Less Toxic Products and Reading Pesticide Labels by Jan Specht 183

CHAPTER 13: INTERACTIONS IN THE GARDEN 187
Insectary Plants Feed Good Bugs by Kathy Reiffenstein 188
Good Bugs for Rose Pests by Jan Specht 191
Diversity in the Garden by Nancy Bauer 194
Plants as Pollution Cleansers by Diane Lynch 196

BAY AREA GARDENS TO VISIT by Maggie Agro 199
AUTHOR BIOGRAPHIES 204
INDEX 206

CHAPTER ONE

Garden Design and Landscaping

Perfect Harmony in Your Garden

~

BY JULIE CARTER, JAN SPECHT AND KATHY REIFFENSTEIN

The jasmine emits its perfumed scent; rich soil sifts through your fingers; the hummingbird hums; the basil tastes spicy and sweet; the roses are a sea of colors. This sensory harmony is nature at work in your garden. Nature has devised a brilliant system of relationships and interdependencies to create this harmony. Knowing a few basics about what happens in your garden and following a few simple practices will help you harness nature's system to work for you.

The World Beneath Our Feet

There is a whole world living and breathing beneath our feet! Good soil is full of earthworms, fungi and bacteria; without all these soil creatures, plants would struggle to grow and survive. Unfortunately, many of the things humans do to the soil degrade the living space of soil organisms and kill them, directly or indirectly. The organisms are starved by our habit of not returning all our garden wastes to the soil as compost. Our tendency to grow the same plants in the same soil year after year provides a monotonous diet for the soil organisms. Pesticides and high nitrogen fertilizers poison them.

Earthworms can produce as much as twenty-five tons of worm castings per acre per year in a temperate climate. This is the Cadillac of fertilizers! Earthworms, along with certain insects, slugs and some snails, burrow through the soil, creating channels that improve aeration and drainage. Beneficial mites, springtails, nematodes and one-celled protozoa are several of the soil organisms that are essential for the optimal release of nutrients to plants, maintenance of good soil structure and control of plant pests. The general rule is that the greater the diversity of soil life, the more fertile the soil.

~ Garden Design and Landscaping ~

To encourage these soil organisms, we need to provide them with organic residues rich in carbon, such as hay, manure or compost. Rich organic compost can also fertilize your plants at the same time. Remember that whenever we eliminate one of these soil organisms, we gardeners get stuck with the jobs they are better equipped to do.

Good Things To Do In Your Garden

Plant the Right Plants in the Right Spot. All plants have specific light and water requirements, so trying to grow a sun-loving plant in the shade is a recipe for pests, disease and failure. When buying a new plant, find out what its needs are: what kind of soil does it like and how much water does it need? Then make sure the location you select in your garden can meet those needs. Examine the plants already in your garden. Are they getting the right amount of sun, shade and water? If they're in the wrong spot, move them. Putting all your plants in the best location to meet their needs will minimize stress and encourage health and vigor.

Choose the Right Plant for our Climate. The Bay area is full of microclimates, but there are some plants that simply do not like our Mediterranean climate of six months wet and six months dry. So, much as you love a favorite plant you grew up with in another area, planting it here will cause it constant stress as it strives to exist in less-than-ideal conditions.

Fertilize Properly. Pests thrive on leaves and buds with high nitrogen levels and frequent fertilizing creates fast, lush growth — just what those hungry pests are after. As well, the more you fertilize, the "thirstier" the plant becomes. Learn how to read a fertilizer label and use a slow release fertilizer. Unless you are treating a specific plant nutrient deficiency, determined by a laboratory test, plants grown in the Bay area need only nitrogen.

Provide the Right Amount of Water. Know what moisture levels your plants need. Both over and under watering stress plants and make them more vulnerable to pest attacks. Either condition can result in yellowing leaves.

Prune Correctly. Dead wood can be removed anytime. Live

branches should be minimally pruned, except during the dormant season. Pruning cuts in the spring and summer on elms, pines, oaks and eucalyptus attract bark beetles and borers that can kill the tree. Pruning can stimulate growth, producing that lush new foliage so attractive to many pests like aphids.

Use the Least Toxic Method of Control. Decide how much pest and disease damage you can tolerate in your garden before it becomes unacceptable or annoying. A few holes in the leaves on your roses may not be reason to call out the big pesticide guns. When you do see some damage on a plant, try to determine exactly what's causing it, and how serious it is. Only when you understand what's creating the problem can you choose the most effective treatment. For example, will you handpick or hose spray the aphids off your new rose growth? Frequent pesticide use may eventually create resistance in the very pests you're trying to eliminate.

Monitor What's Happening in Your Garden. Stroll through your garden frequently and examine the leaves — don't forget the undersides — and flowers of your plants. This will help you catch any problems early, so you'll be able to address them before they're out of control. You'll also have sufficient information to choose the most effective treatment.

Good Bugs and Bad Bugs

Following the above practices will go a long way to giving you a healthy garden, with plants more able to resist insect and disease attacks. But there are still numerous insects that want to feast on your plants.

Luckily for us, Nature has shown her brilliance once again. Beneficial insects, such as lady beetles (ladybugs), green lacewings, parasitic wasps and syrphid flies will feed on the harmful insects that may be damaging your plants. The larvae (immature stage) of the beneficial insects generally provide the best pest control because they are the hungriest. The larvae of syrphid flies eat over sixty aphids in a day. But insect babies rarely look like miniature replicas of their parents, so it's a good idea to identify any insects in your garden before you eliminate them. They might be the good guys!

~ Garden Design and Landscaping ~

Beneficial insects will flock to your garden to help you if you do some simple things to attract them:

- keep your plants healthy by following the above suggestions
- create a favorable environment by planting insectary plants which attract the beneficials
- minimize or eliminate the use of pesticides because beneficials are more readily killed by toxic chemicals
- leave a few "bad" bugs for the beneficials to eat!

Insectary Plants

Most beneficial insects, being relatively small, prefer plants with daisy-like, flat flower clusters because the nectar and pollen are easier to get. Plant these in your garden and watch the good guys appear:

- yarrow (*Achillea millefolium*)
- cosmos (*Cosmos bipinnatus*)
- coriander (*Coriandrum sativum*)
- sunflower (*Helianthus annuus* and *debilis*)
- sweet alyssum (*Lobularia maritima*)
- dill (*Anethum graveolens*)
- fennel (*Foeniculum vulgare*)
- California lilac (*Ceanothus* spp.)

The easy and inexpensive steps above are the fundamentals of a process called Integrated Pest Management, or IPM. IPM encourages you to get to know your garden better and think about the effects of what you do on the complex interrelationships in your garden's ecosystem. It encourages the use of least toxic control methods and more reliance on the natural system that already exists.

So, monitor your garden and who's living there, take care of your soil, encourage the good bugs to come to your garden, use minimal or no toxic pesticides and you'll be helping to maintain that brilliant harmony that is nature.

Principles of Design

by M.C. Dwyer

Gardeners are experts in anticipation. We dream endlessly about creating, changing, and enhancing our environments. In order to achieve our visions we rely on three major principles of design: order, unity and rhythm.

Order

Order is the overall framework of the design, the "big picture" that encompasses its coordinating principles. Order will guide us in making many decisions, such as the selection of an overall theme. Take, for example, the classic Mediterranean design that works well here in the Bay area because of our Mediterranean climate. Following the principle of order ensures that the overall garden looks coherent and feels comfortable.

Creating order includes using balance and even distribution of weight and color. A landscape which has a concentration of large trees and structures situated on one side of the property feels off-balance. Like a heeling boat, it creates a sense of discomfort. To balance the landscape, similarly sized features could be constructed or planted on the other side of the property. Simultaneously, the height or weight of a few of the existing elements could be reduced, for example, by thinning a few trees.

For a more formal look, increase the symmetry of the landscape. Think of planting two exactly matched hedges along a walkway, or placing two of the same pots by your entry. Symmetry illustrates the power of human influence on the garden. On the other hand, an asymmetrical design creates a more casual, natural feeling, where things seem to flow, like a small natural stream meandering along.

Mass is described as groupings of objects. Small shrubs scattered about with lots of distance between them look like a jumble of mounds. To create a better sense of order, join shrubs together to achieve mass. For example, plant larger, similar shrubs in between two smaller shrubs to crease a mass of shrubs with emphasis on the center taller point; or transplant or buy more of the same small shrubs and combine them with the existing scattered shrubs, creating several groups. Alternatively, connect the existing shrubs into groups by using several pots of one new plant. This would still create mass, while adding the element of the containers for variety.

Unity

Unity provides a sense of oneness and harmony. Unity is achieved through color, size, texture and shape. A monochromatic garden is an example of unity. Trees often have a particular shape to their natural growth pattern, such as columns of yew trees, pyramids of cedars, and the cloud-like shape of many oaks. Selecting annuals and perennials with shapes similar to existing trees will add unity to the garden design. Another wonderful opportunity to create unity lies in selecting and grouping plants with specific textures: wispy grasses, lacy artemesia or sword-like iris.

Unity can be accomplished by installing a dominant feature as a focal point, such as a statue, rock outcropping, fountain, or a larger plant within a group of smaller plants. In a sunny area, select a favorite annual, such as the long-blooming cosmos, and group smaller varieties of cosmos around a dominant core of taller cosmos.

Unity is supported by interconnection. Create outlines or connecting lines that visually tie elements together. Borders are a common way of achieving interconnection, as are walkways between different garden rooms.

The "Unity of Three" principle says that groups of three things together have a particular visual appeal. The eye tends to divide a group of two in half, while a group of four looks odd and would be better reduced to three. In general, odd numbers of things look best to the human eye.

Rhythm

Rhythm implies timing and movement. Rhythm is achieved through the use of repetition, like the familiar refrain or chorus in a song. In the garden, repeating hardscapes, such as using the same type of stepping stone throughout, creates rhythm. Or, employ the principle of alternation by placing a different stone every once in a while. Alternation is also a useful device for breaking the monotony of a long fence or wall. Inversion, or a complete change of pattern, such as laying deck boards in a new pattern, is valuable to visually indicate a cross road, turning point, or especially a height change along a walking route.

Employ gradation in your garden by gradually changing a pattern, perhaps by increasing sizes. For example, you can ease a transition from a horizontal front lawn to a vertical two-story home by gradually increasing the heights of the plant materials you use in a border between the lawn and the home.

Color

In addition to order, unity and rhythm, color is an important element of design. Colors suggest mood and energy level. Generally, the more energetic and stimulating colors are warmer, ranging from yellows through reds, while the more meditative, calmer, cooler colors are blues and greens. To brighten and warm up a shady area, add plants with cream and yellow variegated leaves, like hostas or red flowers like fuchsias. To cool down a hot spot, consider plants like lavender or light blue asters.

To coordinate the colors of your garden with the colors of your home, take paint swatches with you to the nursery. Stick with two or three colors of similar intensity. Match pale flowers with pale paint, or deeply colored flowers with a rich color paint. Or, add contrast and vitality by using one color of the opposite intensity to your house paint, such as a richly purple flowering bush against a soft yellow paint.

Think Fire Safe Landscaping

BY DIANE LYNCH

Wildfires rage throughout the west during summer. As fires have burned large areas, the rest of the west has continued to dry out, creating more fuel for future fires. In parts of the Bay area, dead and dying oaks add to the problem.

Wildland fires are part of many ecosystems in the west. Proper landscaping can minimize this threat in populated areas. As more and more exotic plants have been introduced to the Bay area, we have changed the nature of a wildfire from a low intensity fire useful to the land to a potential blaze of catastrophic proportions. Picture towering eucalyptus torches and then envision the changes in soil chemistry that result. These can affect the way soil absorbs water after a eucalyptus fire.

The Oakland fire of 1991 and the Mt. Vision fire in Inverness in 1995 both occurred in October, which can be the Bay area's most troublesome month: warm, windy and very dry, just before the winter rains. The Oakland fire destroyed over 3400 homes. Unfortunately, Marin is ripe for a similar conflagration as the fuel load on Mt. Tamalpais alone is estimated to be three times that of the Oakland hills before the fire. All it takes is a windy, dry day and a spark. Firefighters, when faced with a large fire, will select the most defensible properties and let others, considered too dangerous because of terrain, architectural features, or landscaping, go.

PYROPHYTES

Pyrophytes are plants that ignite readily and burn intensely. Certain characteristics will frequently be found in plants that are volatile. Pyrophytes characteristically:

- have leaves that are stiff, woody, small, fine/lacey, or needle-like
- contain volatile oils, fats, waxes
- are aromatic when crushed; sap is gummy, resinous, odorous
- have loose or papery bark and other dry leaves/brush

Plants that are considered most flammable include dry annual grasses, anything with excessive deadwood, dried or cured herbs, any plantings that are overly dense or under stress. Natives are usually considered good landscaping plants because of their ability to withstand drought, but some natives are quite flammable when not irrigated. These include chamise (*Adenostoma fasciculatum*), coyote brush (*Baccharis*), California sagebrush (*Artemisia californica*), black sage (*Salvia mellifera*) tan oak (*Lithocarpus densiflora*), California bay (*Umbellularia californica*) and many pines (*Pinus* spp.). Many of the noxious weeds are very volatile: pampas and jubata grass (*Cortaderia* spp.), acacia, eucalyptus, brooms (*Cytisus & Spartium* spp.). Other hazardous plants include firs (*Abies* spp.), bamboo (*Bambusa* spp.), cedars (*Cedrus* spp.), junipers (*Juniperus* spp.) and spruces (*Picea* spp.).

Think of everything you plant as potential fuel and take into account prevailing winds, especially if you live on a hill. Dry grasses and shrubs can ignite easily and winds can push a fire directly up toward a home very quickly. Overhanging branches should be trimmed away from the house, vegetation kept thinned, and plants irrigated. We are encouraged to plant with periodic drought in mind but, from a fire safety standpoint, some summer water is a good strategy because a plant with water in its tissues will be less flammable. Unwatered plants will be dry and flammable. Mulch is necessary to retain water, but it is best to use a wood chip mulch as opposed to shredded bark which can ignite easily if a cigarette is pitched into it. Understory shrubs are best kept under two feet tall and not too densely planted.

Fire-Resistant Plants

Fire-resistant plants tend to have leaves that are supple and easily crushed and watery, odorless sap. Many are broadleaf, deciduous trees

Garden Design and Landscaping

that tend to be clean, not bushy, with little deadwood. Others are low growing shrubs and taller shrubs with minimal dead, bushy material.

Among the most fire resistant plants available are the succulents such as ice plants (many varieties, some of which are invasive and should not be used near the coast), hens and chicks (*Escheveria* spp.), sedums and aloes. Most succulents require little summer water. Many native trees and shrubs are fire resistant: buckeye (*Aesculus californica*), alders (*Alnus* spp.), pacific dogwood (*Cornus nuttalli*), oaks (*Quercus* spp.), willows (*Salix* spp.), coast redwood (*Sequoia sempervirens*), some *Ceanothus*, toyon (*Heteromeles arbutifolia*), some manzanita (*Arctostaphylos* spp.) and rockrose (*Cistus* spp.).

Many commonly used exotic trees and shrubs are safe to plant: maple *(Acer* spp.), citrus, *Myoporum*, mock orange *(Pittosporum* spp.), *Escallonia* spp., privets (*Ligustrum* spp.), oleander (*Nerium oleander*), butterfly bush (*Buddleia* spp.), *Cotoneaster* spp., *Lavatera* spp., lavender (*Lavandula* spp.) and *Lantana* spp. Dozens of perennials and groundcovers are good bets: *Liviope* spp., *Santolina* spp., *Pelargonium* spp., *Geranium* spp., *Vinca* spp., *Agapanthus* spp., *Heuchera* spp., *Penstemon* spp., *Iris* spp., lambs ears (*Stachys byzantina*), California fuchsia (*Zauschneria californica*), common calla (*Zantedeschia aethiopica*).

Fall is a great time to rework your landscape. New plants will have the benefit of the winter rains to become established and you can improve your garden from a fire safety standpoint by removing selected pyrophytes and putting in fire-resistant plants.

Feng Shui in the Garden

by Terumi Leinow

Gardeners and feng shui have a lot in common. Gardeners work with the earth and thank heaven for rain and sun. Feng shui is about that balance of earth (yin) and heaven (yang). Gardeners are attuned to the cycles of life. We rejoice at new growth and birth in spring, enjoy the fruits of our labor in summer, savor the autumn harvest and put things to bed in winter. Feng shui translates those cycles into five elements:

- wood (spring) represents new growth and connection to family
- fire (summer) fuels our presence and reputation in the world
- metal (autumn) symbolizes creativity and children
- water (winter) represents the flow of opportunities that translate into career
- earth teaches us about relationship and nourishment

Our gardens teach us about harmony, balance and beauty and are a haven of serenity and joy. The garden is also the greatest producer of chi — life force energy. Harmony, balance, beauty, serenity, chi is feng shui!

Water

The shui in feng shui means water. Water symbolizes wisdom and the harvesting of wealth. Water shows us our life path and brings good fortune. Position your fountain close to the front door of your home as the front door is considered the receiver of chi. Life from the outside world comes to you through the front door. Therefore, having a water feature near the entrance and directing the flow of water towards the door keeps chi, the vital life force, activated. Ensure that the pathway to your front door is easy to access, uncluttered and attractive.

Wealth

Black Sect Tantric Buddhism (BTB) feng shui was introduced to America by Grand Master Lin Yun and is the most widely practiced system of feng shui in the United States. He is the world's foremost authority on feng shui. According to BTB feng shui, the wealth corner of a property, home, room or garden is determined by the entrance to these areas. Therefore, stand in the main entrance to your garden. From here, the farthest left corner of the garden would be the area associated with wealth. To enhance this area, consider planting an orange or persimmon tree that is considered auspicious as both represent good luck. The color purple is also associated with wealth, so lilac, orchid tree, Mexican sage, hydrangeas, salvia superba, and platycodons are additional good choices. The wealth corner is also a good location for a water feature, a gazing ball, or a large urn to receive prosperity. Regarding trees in general, avoid planting the bad luck mulberry tree. Evergreen trees are preferable to deciduous and upward-growing are better than downward. Flowering and fruit bearing trees, such as peach, apple and pear are also good.

Rocks

Rocks are important features in the feng shui garden. Chinese and Japanese gardens attempt to replicate nature and recreate miniature landscapes in the garden. Rocks evoke the presence and power of the mountain and a series of smooth stones along a path can simulate the river. Rocks also add texture, power and stability to a garden. If you have a special rock in mind, be like the sculptor who sees the image in the material — tune in to the essence of the rock, see what it evokes and develop your theme accordingly.

Rock Garden Chic

~

by Stacy Nelson

One of the most beautiful rock gardens I have ever seen is right next door. My neighbor's son, who is a priest in Brazil, put it all together and likes to help maintain it. This rock garden works very well for many reasons—it is low maintenance, drought tolerant and inspiringly gorgeous.

Placement

The best rock gardens are located on slopes, banks and small valleys. Analyze your house and garden carefully for scale to determine the size and number of rocks that will be most appropriate for your location. Mediterranean or Spanish style houses seem particularly well-suited to rock gardens. Place large rocks first at the low parts of a slope and work upward, clustering the rocks as you go. Slope the top of the rocks backward to direct rainwater to the roots of the plants. Ensure naturalness by using all the same types of rocks throughout your garden. Also look at the stratification on the lines on the rocks to make sure they are all going the same way. Arrange rocks at your desired location reflecting on natural rock formations you have seen. Having just returned from Yosemite National Park, I saw many rock formations to inspire! Rocks should not be sticking straight out of the ground. Bury your rocks one-quarter or half way down in the soil to ensure a natural effect.

Create rock garden terraces by stacking rocks facing backward. Cement the rocks in place with soil that allows you to place plants like creeping thyme or succulents along, as well as in, the stone crevices. Use single plants for points of special interest or color, such as Japanese maples or conifers.

~ *Garden Design and Landscaping* ~

Selecting Plants

Plants appropriate for your rock garden are likely to include ones that thrive under harsher conditions, like native grasses. Consider drifts of plants that flow like water down a hill or plants that stand tall and blow gracefully in the wind like *Pennisetum setaceum* 'Rubrum', otherwise known as red fountain grass. Planting sages and lavender together creates a purple haze. *Teucrium* or germander will also blend well into this grouping as a sage gray colored large shrub. *Rosmarinus officinalis* 'Blue Spires' will add evergreen and definition to your rock garden. *Berberis* or barberry is a brilliant plant that is dark reddish brown in color and is a great focal point shrub in-between evergreen shrubs. Add *Achillea* 'Moonshine' or yarrow for a glow of deep yellow. Rhododendrons will offer a blast of color in the spring and penstemon will outlast the summer with colors in garnet, purple, pink or white. The shrub, *Hebe*, created a lot of interest at a recent designer's show I attended because of its beautiful delicate flowers framed in dark green foliage. Carpet the garden below the rocks with low plants or with plants that can flow out of pockets in a rock wall. Try scented plants that brush against your ankles and smell sweetly of mint or thyme. Sedum also makes a wonderful ground or bank cover in a rock garden. To maintain your rock garden, cut back your perennials as well as the grasses when they dry out. Check rock wall plantings and crevices for proper drainage and irrigation.

Benches and Birdbaths

Adding special interest and focal points enhances any garden. Make a Zen-inspired rock bench with a flat long rock and two medium rocks underneath for meditating. Select rocks that collect water in a dip in the rock to provide a bath for your birds. Create a trough by placing stones in a rectangle and use a pond liner to create a water feature. Construct a rock stairway with square cutouts where you can grow succulents like *Echeveria* (hen and chicks) and *Aeonium urbicum*.

Greenhouses

∼

BY MAGGIE AGRO

Erecting a greenhouse is much like falling down Alice's rabbit hole. It leads you to exciting new possibilities in gardening that allow you to grow almost anything you desire, in any season, and its planning opens up a dizzying new world of information.

As a health spa for your plants, a greenhouse provides optimum warmth and moisture year around. When the sun's warmth collects inside a greenhouse, moisture from the plants and on the floors condenses and creates moist vapor. Vents and fans allow heat to escape and fresh air to enter. Feeding and watering is consistent and can be adjusted for different areas according to plants' requirements. Your plants thrive and flourish, and you have freshly cut flowers, herbs and vegetables for your table throughout the year.

But, how do you choose the right location and type of greenhouse for your property? Will you build it yourself or hire a contractor? What should you look for? What upkeep and operating costs are involved? How do you begin?

A greenhouse should be located in a spot that receives at least six hours of sunlight per day, year around, to maximize the warmth and light of the sun and to reduce the amount of heat and light that you have to provide. Over years of operation, a sunny location can save you a lot of money. You need an area with good drainage and proximity to water, electrical hookups, storage and a composting area.

If you can satisfy the environmental requirements, then check with your local planning board to make sure you can build, and to find out if design and setback ordinances are involved. If you can attach the greenhouse to your home and tie into existing utilities, you can lower construction costs. If you plan to use it for sitting or enter-

~ Garden Design and Landscaping ~

taining, you will limit its function as a greenhouse because it will need to be cooler and dryer, and it may become taxable as additional living space to your home.

Freestanding greenhouses can be very flexible in size and shape and can be adjusted for different terrains, but they require their own heating and cooling systems and water supply. They can make a stunning architectural statement or they can be entirely functional and inexpensive. They can be built from scratch or they can be ordered in kit form with all parts pre-cut and pre-drilled, or with materials for you to cut and drill. A more finished kit is more expensive, but don't forget to add your time and aggravation as a cost in a basic, no-frills kit. Also, make sure that the kit you choose meets any building codes and that electrical and plumbing hookups meet local standards for safe operation.

If you decide to buy a kit, make comparisons in different kits for the weight of the frame and the gauge of the materials, and whether doors are pre-hung and ventilation is included. Look for UV protection and durability of covering material for your climate, rust proofing, hardware, add-ons for heating and cooling, benches, warranties, and freight or delivery to your site. You may find some options are cheaper from other suppliers but make sure their installation in another vendor's product does not invalidate warranty.

A difficult assembly may require you to pay someone to help you. You need strength for heavy manual work like digging a foundation and pouring concrete, carrying and spreading bags of gravel or laying flagstone, carrying lumber or metal struts, assembling and raising walls, and mounting fans. You need skills for basic carpentry, wiring and plumbing, too.

If you decide to build from the ground up, you will need a good plan. You can purchase a book of plans or have one designed for you by a contractor. If there are difficulties with the site, hiring a professional can often prevent costly mistakes and save you time and money. And you can always build in stages if the initial outlay seems too high.

For an easy start, Ortho Books' *All About Greenhouses* features several basic plans including the simple, inexpensive, hoop-design greenhouse that you often see at large nurseries. Constructed with basic tools, the frame consists of posts of one and one-half inch galvanized pipe and lengths of PVC pipe whose ends will fit snugly into the galvanized pipe. The frame is covered with eight millimeter UV protected film and requires only basic skills and strength to assemble. It isn't very pretty to look at it, can't tolerate high winds, but offers adequate protection for the Bay area's mild winter.

Inside, you need racks and hangers for plants, and rustproof plant benches, some equipped with thermostatically controlled heating cables and misting systems for rooting and sprouting. You can save money on heating costs by keeping your temperature around fifty degrees at night and by providing heating cables to seedlings and young plants if you are propagating. Landscaping around your greenhouse with low-growing shrubs helps to insulate and reduce heating costs.

A greenhouse can have many hidden costs. Thorough research, with a study of several publications and visits to various websites, can help you understand all that is involved. A trip to small-scale local nurseries with greenhouses may yield some good tips from commercial growers for saving money and operating efficiently.

CHAPTER TWO

Climate and Your Garden

Mediterranean Climates and What They Mean to Us

∼

by Diane Lynch

Looking for interesting plants that will survive the next drought, when your neighbors will have brown lawns? Think California natives and plants from other Mediterranean climates around the world.

There are five regions in the world that have so-called Mediterranean climates. They are characterized by their locations on the western sides of continents thirty to forty degrees from the equator and by dry summers and wet, mild winters. Interestingly, the western edges of the continents have cold offshore currents and a complex phenomenon called upwelling. Upwelling makes these ocean areas very rich and varied in life forms and also moderates the summer temperatures in coastal areas. The reason the Bay area has rain in the winter months and not in the summer months is due to its location between two major climate zones. The northwest zone brings rain to the Seattle area most of the year, but affects the Bay area mostly in the winter months. The southern California zone is dry and calm and dominates the Bay area's summer weather. Other areas of the world that have similar climates are the southwestern tip of Africa, portions of western Australia, the central coast of Chile, and, of course, the Mediterranean basin, which has the world's largest area with this type of climate. The amounts of rainfall and length of dry spells vary considerably within each of these regions. Summer drought is the defining factor but it can range from eleven to twelve months down to one or two months.

Because we in the Bay area share these common characteristics with other parts of the world, we have a rich source of exotic plants that will do well in our climate because they evolved in similar conditions. In fact, some of our most commonly grown plants came from other Mediterranean areas.

From Chile we have *Alstroemeria*, called Peruvian Lily, an easy-to-grow perennial. The common garden nasturtium, *Tropaeolum majus*, originated in Chile as well as the interesting conifer *Araucaria araucana*, or monkey puzzle tree. *Gunnera tinctoria* or *chilensis*, also known as pangue or dinosaur food, is native to stream banks, has enormous prickly leaves and needs consistent moisture. Young stems are peeled and eaten as a treat. Some species of *Podocarpus*, landscape trees, *Maytenus boaria*, the mayten tree used widely in California, as well as *Fuchsia magellanica*, pollinated by hummingbirds, also originated in Chile.

South Africa has given us many wonderful plants such as the scented geraniums, *Pelargonium* species, which grow very large in their native settings, bloom most of the year and have many interesting scents and uses. The ubiquitous calla lily, *Zantedeschia aethiopica*, not actually in the lily family, is native to South Africa. So are lily-of-the-Nile, *Agapanthus* species; red hot poker, *Kniphofias* species; and some *Gladiolus* species. The widely grown African daisy, *Osteospermun* species, also called freeway daisy, is used as groundcover throughout much of California.

Australia's southwestern Mediterranean areas are rich in plants used extensively in California, some of which are considered invasive because they have impolitely reproduced. For instance, there are over three hundred species of eucalyptus, four hundred species of acacias and two hundred species of grevillea, many of which grow well in the Bay area. The bottlebrush shrubs, *Callistemon* species, that attract hummingbirds are in the same myrtle family as eucalyptus. Interestingly, some introduced species from other Mediterranean areas have become invasive problems in Australia. *Gladiolus caryophyllaceus*, for instance, is endangered in its native South Africa but has become an aggressive weed in southwestern Australia. Man has been moving plants around the globe for several hundred years. In many areas, native plants have suffered as exotics (introduced species) have been brought in and, in some cases, taken over large areas at the expense of the local flora.

The Mediterranean basin is a larger, more complex area than the other Mediterranean climates. It spans southern Europe from Spain to Turkey and the Balkan peninsula and east to Israel and Lebanon. Egypt and Libya are excluded as desert climates, but the north African countries of Morocco, Algeria and Tunisia are included. Because of the variety of climatic conditions in this vast area, plant life is similarly varied. Many of our food crops are native to the Mediterranean basin: lentils, chick peas, beans, cabbage, asparagus, artichokes, leeks, figs, grapes, olives, almonds, wheat and barley. Other foods we associate with Europe were actually imports: tomatoes, corn and peppers were from the western hemisphere and oranges and lemons originated in eastern Asia. Among the decorative plants native to the Mediterranean basin are *Iris* species; *Lavandula* species, lavenders; *Nerium oleander*; *Myrtus communis*, true myrtle; *Narcissus* species, daffodil and narcissus; *Quercus suber*, cork oak; *Rosmarinus officinalis*, rosemary; *Tulipa* species, tulip; *Cistus* species, rock rose; and *Cyclamen* species.

How Many Climates in Your Garden?

∼

BY MAGGIE AGRO

A lot of us have a hard time figuring out what climatic zone we are in, and when we ask for assistance at nurseries, saying that we live in Sausalito or Novato does not give the whole picture. Climate varies drastically from Point Reyes to Novato to the Golden Gate. More importantly, it even changes from one area of your garden to another. These many areas of different climates are called microclimates. If you don't take time to get acquainted with the microclimates in your garden, despite your hard work, you may suffer disappointment.

As newcomers to the Bay area several years ago, we acquired a house with little else but ivy and baby tears. I went immediately to the nursery—this was before I had studied to become a Master Gardener—and asked for help by giving their expert what I thought was good information about my garden: I live in Sausalito. I came home with a trunk load of plants, about 20% of which survived. Why?

I did not understand the complexity of Bay area climates. I failed to notice that on one side of my house, my patio collects cool air that drops from higher lots above and behind us. I encounter frost damage only on that patio. Plants tend to grow less or develop a leggy growth habit and bloom less there, too. Further down on the same side of the house, the soil is always damp, fed by an underground spring and sheltered by large, established evergreen trees. On the other side of our house, I find dry shade at one end and dry sun at the other.

I don't need to rely on the advice of a horticulturist. I need to do my homework. Homework includes spending time in my garden at different times of the day in different types of weather. Because certain microclimatic limitations may prevent plants from attaining their maximum growth, I need to identify sections of the garden with too much or too little light, water, temperature and wind, in order to select the right plant for the right place. Microclimatic conditions can cause stress that leads to outbreaks of diseases, insect pests, and decline.

Getting to know a garden is like getting to know a person. It is attention to detail that creates an intimate relationship. Without this understanding, my gardening is just a series of random activities.

To become intimate with a garden, one must consider several factors. Western coastal gardens have a milder climate than those inland because of the warming effect of the ocean. During summer, the ocean absorbs and retains heat from the sun and lowers temperatures around it. In the winter, the ocean releases solar energy to warm the air giving us mild, wet weather. These dry summers and wet winters are characteristic of a Mediterranean climate.

Though Bay area winters are milder than winters in most of the United States, you must still know the low winter temperatures of your garden in order to protect plants from frost damage. Cold air sinks and tends to pool in low places, almost like water. Fences and houses can act as dams and cause this cold air to collect. Slopes don't collect cold air because cold air drains off them. You probably know where these areas are, intuitively, because they aren't usually the places you like to sit and enjoy your garden. You can find these warm or cold pockets by walking your garden on cold mornings and looking for white frost spots or melted plants. Choose frost resistant plants for these areas.

Try to notice when and where your garden gets the most sunlight. Observe where you have gentle morning sun and harsh afternoon sun. Because the location where the sun rises and sets is always changing, a part of the garden shaded in the early spring may become very hot as the sun slides into summer. During summer, we get more direct sunlight because the sun rises and sets almost directly above us. In winter, sunlight shines on us at a greater angle, rising and setting from farther south. If you watch where the sun rises and sets at the beginning of each month, you will understand how seasonal changes relate to the angle of the sun. You will also see that plants are dormant when shad-

~ Climate and Your Garden ~

ows are longer. Heavy growth occurs with more sunlight and some plants require more sunlight than others to bear fruit or flowers.

On windy days, move around your garden and feel the force of the wind in different areas. The movement of air can heat and dry out soil and foliage. Where winds are heavy and unhampered, plants can be twisted by their drying effect. Storms can pull and tear trees to shreds. Observe how wind affects your garden. Notice that narrow areas tend to funnel the air and intensify it. You can try to either promote or control its effects by constructing or removing barriers. Barriers should be constructed to slow the air, not obstruct it entirely. Fences with basket weave or shrubs are good ways to tame the wind.

Look for signs of rot or fungus and mildew. During winter months, fog rises from the damp, warm soils inland. At the coast, fogs ebb and flow on a daily basis so that afternoons may be sunny, with fog returning during the night. These conditions foster mildew and fungus diseases, which become difficult to control if there is insufficient air movement. Roses, which thrive in sunny areas, may show more signs of disease in an area where air circulation is poor.

Take note of areas near your plants. Beds next to south and west facing walls can be subject to hotter conditions than other areas in your garden. In the warm months, plants and lawns near paving can be burned by dry heat radiating from hot pavement and walls. But, during the winter, a reflective wall or pavement may radiate enough heat to warm plants in an otherwise cool area. Place drought resistant plants near hot driveways and pavement and paint dark walls with a light color to radiate heat in cool areas. You can buy large mirrors at tag sales and place them in shaded areas. If arranged artfully, they add light to dark areas and provide a sense of depth.

You can learn much about your garden by observation, but the real benefit is the kinship you develop with your surroundings. With every moment that you sit in your garden as an observer, you will have more success and fewer failures, and you will have the satisfaction of knowing why it all works.

Made for the Shade

~

by Maggie Agro

Every garden has some shade. If your home has a north side, or if the sapling you planted is now a mature tree, you have shade. And no matter what folks tell you, shade is a good thing. Many plants thrive in the shade, and it's that lush, cool respite from the heat that draws us to a woodland setting. Muir Woods is always cool and teeming with vegetation.

A lot of people claim that their plants always die in the shade, but the shade isn't the problem, it's the soil. If the shade is under trees, remember that a tree's roots are hungry and will devour all of the nutrients and water. Soil around trees often becomes hard and lifeless as a result. You've got to revive and replenish that soil with lots of humus, decomposed organic matter. It can be compost, sterilized and well-rotted manure, shredded leaf mold (last year's leaves), peat moss, and decomposed kitchen waste like coffee grounds and vegetable waste.

Think about the floor of a forest with the leaves and decaying matter that cover it. Humus lightens the soil and holds water and eventually becomes part of the soil. It's a good reason to start a compost heap if you haven't already. If you get leaf mulch from your city's recycling plant, be sure to let it sit as compost for at least three to four months before you use it, in order to kill any weed seeds and roots it might contain.

A good way to determine if your soil needs humus is to dig a hole about ten inches deep and fill it with water. If the water isn't absorbed almost immediately, your soil is either hard-pack clay or already too wet. The cure is the same for both. Add plenty of humus, try to work in at least one inch of the present soil and try not to walk on the area.

~ Climate and Your Garden ~

If it is a walkway, install stepping stones. Another way to tell if your soil has enough humus is to look for the presence of worms. If it's without worms, you need more humus.

You can also buy a home-testing kit to determine the acidity and nutrient level of your soil. Directions are included and will tell you that neutral is a pH of seven. Below seven is acidic, sometimes called sour. Above seven is alkaline, sometimes called sweet. Shade should fall between five point five and six point five. Leaf mold or composted pine needles can acidify soil and lime can sweeten it.

A shade garden should be damp all of the time. An underground drip irrigation system or a soaker hose will pay off in the long run. Over time it will conserve water because it puts the water at the roots and minimizes runoff. It will prevent wet flowers and foliage, a good breeding ground for disease.

You can modify light by careful pruning of trees to let the light through. You can cut limbs that grow too close to the ground to provide more light and enhance air circulation. Prune shrubs from within to thin out the middle and allow air to circulate and light to penetrate.

If you plant under trees, try to plant near the drip line, as roots may be too large nearer the trunk. Don't rototill because tree roots grow close to the surface. Cutting smaller roots won't hurt, but use a sharp spade or lopping shears to avoid tearing them.

Another important consideration is the type of shade that you have. There are many degrees of shade:

- partial shade, at its most sunny, might get two hours of sunshine a day
- light shade would be an area that gets cooler, early morning sun or warmer, late afternoon sun
- filtered light is in the shadow cast by a small-leaved tree or a lath covering
- in bright light, no direct rays come into the garden, but the space is open to the sky, like the north side of the house

- dappled shade comes from larger-leaved trees and is true or full shade; even full shade gets strong light (not direct sun) thirty percent of the day
- deep shade is close to a north-facing wall or under a dense canopy of trees and shrubs; plants cannot grow in complete shade because they need light to manufacture chlorophyll—so, if you have dense shade and plants are growing there, it is getting light from reflection off a white wall or filtered through a tree's branches.

When you look into purchasing plants or observing them in the wild, you will find that the foliage and overall form of shade plants is their strongest feature. When making your selections, vary leaf shape and color. In deep shade, try using silvers and light greens to brighten up dark spots. Give the eye a tapestry of shape, texture, and varied greens. When you look into a well-planned shade garden, you discover the play of broad leaves with small leaves, round with angular, light with dark.

There are some wildflowers that work well and, usually, reproduce themselves. The only drawback with wildflowers is that most die back in the winter. Some good choices are: Solomon's seal, baneberry, bishop's cap, Dutchman's breeches, fringed bleeding heart, bloodroot, iris cristata, jack-in-the-pulpit, lady's slipper, trillium, many varieties of violets, wild geraniums, and wild ginger.

A surefire way to find plants that will work well in your type of shade is to walk your neighborhood and look for shady areas in neighbors' gardens or buy only one of a plant and audition it in your garden for a few seasons.

Drought Tolerant Ferns

~

BY BARBARA J. EUSER

Drought tolerant ferns—isn't that an oxymoron? When I think of ferns, I think of cool, damp spaces, shade, the sound of a creek gently burbling. That image is certainly true. Ferns do grow best in the shade. But it is also true that some species of ferns do not require a constant source of water. Hiking in our state parks, I have noted the profusion of a number of different species of ferns, growing lushly despite lack of artificial watering throughout the dry summer months.

In my own garden, I have planted sword ferns, the California native *Polystichum munitum*, among the most common drought tolerant ferns. They thrive in the shade next to the east wall of our house. One large fern has grown and expanded and is begging to be divided. I am waiting until the fall rains start. That way, the newly divided plants will benefit from our natural wet weather to reestablish their roots and will be prepared for next summer's dryness.

Although sword ferns commonly grow under redwoods in natural forests, they need little water once established. Sword ferns are also suitable for growing under oaks, which is to say, they are drought tolerant. Sword ferns are widespread in the Bay area's open spaces, from deep forests to open hillsides. Regarding deer resistance, my own observation is that sword ferns are not the first choice of the deer that forage in my garden. However, the deer have neatly clipped the tender tips of some of the smaller ferns under our bay tree. The longer, tougher fronds are apparently not as palatable, and I think the sword ferns will survive without added protection.

There are a number of species of native California ferns sufficiently drought tolerant to be suitable for growing under coast live oak (*Quercus agrifolia*) and Valley Oak (*Q. lobata*) trees. As our native oaks are susceptible to crown rot and oak root fungus, it is important that any plants under oaks not require much summer water.

In describing ferns, three terms are useful: fern leaves are called fronds, the leaflets of a frond are called pinnae, and the reproductive clusters along the margins of the leaf or lobes are called sori.

- California Maidenhair Fern (*Adiantum jordanii*) has stiff, wire-like stems lined with tiny, green fan-shaped leaflets or pinnae. It is native to southern Oregon and California. Growing as high as two feet tall, it has a delicate appearance consistent with its common name.
- Coffee Fern (*Pellaea andromedifolia*) is a small plant, growing to eighteen inches high. Unlike many ferns that have dark green foliage, the coffee fern's fronds range from gray-green to bluish-green. Its native habitat is southern Oregon and California. Although it doesn't need much water to survive, it may look dry during the summer months without occasional irrigation.
- Bird's Foot Fern (*Pellaea mucronata*) is related to—that is, in the same genus as—the Coffee Fern. It is larger than the Coffee Fern and derives its name from its distinctive foliage that consists of narrow leaflets arranged in groups of three. With some imagination, the fern's leaflets mirror the tracks of birds left in the sand.
- California Gold Back Fern (*Pentagramma triangularis*) has shiny brown or black stems with two to five inch fronds. Its pinnae are bright green above with a golden yellow underside, giving the fern its common name. The edges of the leaflets are slightly turned back which produce a three-dimensional effect. Dense, dark black sori contrast with the golden undersides.
- Bracken Fern (*Pteridium aquilinum*), a course, rough-looking fern, is native to many parts of the world. To me, it conjures up references to wind-swept moors in English novels. But it is also native to California. In Marin, I have seen it growing in

thick patches as tall as four feet, although it may grow almost twice that high under some conditions. It is suitable for a garden with a natural, untamed look. It spreads by its deep rootstocks, and is reputed to be potentially invasive. Some sources warn that the young fronds of bracken are not to be gathered to cook as fiddleheads: they are a slow poison.

- California Polypody (*Polypodium californicum*) are small ferns with fronds up to fifteen inches long. In the wild, they live in small clusters, sticking out of crevices or popping up along trails. The pinnae have smooth rounded tips and, on their undersides, the sori form two rows.
- Leather Leaf Fern (*Polypodium scouleri*) is the fern commonly used in flower arrangements. It is long lasting and conveys the impression of natural woodlands in the vase indoors. Leather Leaf Fern is native from British Columbia to California. Its natural habitat is on trees and rocks, or growing in clumps in leaf mold in soil. It spreads by short rhizomes and will naturalize in the garden.
- California Wood Fern (*Dryopteris arguta*) is native all along the western coast from Washington to southern California. It may grow nearly three feet tall with wide spreading fronds that sway in the breeze. The pinnae remind me of many tiny oak leaves attached to a single long stem. It is a large, attractive fern, but may be difficult to grow in the garden.
- Licorice Fern (*Polypodium glycyrrhiza*), another California native, resembles a small version of the sword fern (*Polystichum munitum*) above. According to Donald Kirk's book, *Wild Edible Plants*, "the stem of the leaf, when chewed long enough, develops a distinct licorice flavor."

These ten species of ferns are all California natives with low water requirements. All are suitable for use in Bay area gardens. By planting a selection of these shade-loving ferns, a feeling of lushness and native woodlands can grace any garden in the Bay area.

CHAPTER THREE

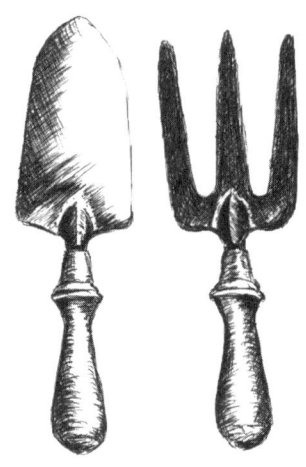

Soil, Its Composition and Health

The "Dirt" on Soil

~

by Diane Lynch

Dirt is what you sweep up in the house. Soil is an amalgam of living organisms, decaying plant matter and decomposing minerals that are literally the foundation of your garden. It is easy to oversimplify the soil in the garden because most of what makes it so complex is invisible to the naked eye. Most roots are in the top six to twelve inches of soil and this is a constantly changing environment of bacteria, fungi, and other microscopic organisms. In the Bay area we are blessed with a moderate climate that allows us to grow almost anything. Ironically, that climate contributes to one of our biggest challenges: heavy clay soil.

Ideal garden soil would be a sandy loam of forty percent sand, forty percent silt, twenty percent clay. Throw in five to fifteen percent organic matter and, in theory, you'd have perfection. Since few of us have that perfect situation, we can improve soil structure by adding organic matter, either in the form of mulch on top, or incorporated into the soil. In sandy soil, organic material will trap water making it available longer to plant roots; in clay soil, it will open the soil up, making it easier to work and improving drainage by opening up air passages. Adding fertilizer might seem like a good way to improve fertility and, while it is true that plants can't distinguish between chemical and organic forms of fertilizer, only organic amendments will improve soil structure. It's usually better to err on the side of "less is more" when it comes to chemical fertilizer application for two reasons: excess fertilizer can burn plant roots, and in the Bay area, excess fertilizer demands more watering which will leach nitrates and will end up in our treasured Bay, upsetting balances there.

Adding organic amendments is an ongoing process, not a one-shot solution. Changes to soil will not occur overnight, but over a couple of years the improvement can be dramatic. Some publications will recommend adding sand to clay soil but this is never a good idea because if the proportions aren't right you can combine the soil particles in such a way that your soil will literally turn to concrete.

Soil Particles

There are three basic types of soil particles:

- Sand, the largest particle, feels gritty and will form a ball in your hand when moist, but the ball crumbles when touched. Because there is a lot of airspace between the grains, drainage in sand is so excellent that plants need frequent watering and nutrients can be leached out as a result. Medium sand has about six thousand particles per gram and can be seen with the naked eye.
- Silt has much smaller particles than sand, 6 million per gram, and when moist, can be pressed together readily but crumbles when dry.
- Clay has over ninety million particles per gram that can only be seen individually with an electron microscope! These particles are so tightly packed that when you water or it rains, it takes a long time for the water to penetrate; but once in there, it also takes a long time to dry out, which can cause plants to drown, due to lack of adequate oxygen for the roots. When wet clay is squeezed between thumb and forefinger, it will slither out as a ribbon which can get quite long before breaking. Clay soils tend to be rich in nutrients, but challenging to manage.

Managing Clay Soils

Clay soils require different treatment, depending on the season. Without some summer water, our clay soils will dry up and large

～ Soil, Its Composition and Health ～

cracks will open up by mid-summer. Using a soaker hose or sprinkler over a period of several hours, irrigate until an inch or two per square foot of water infiltrates the soil to a depth of twelve inches. After the area is damp, mulching with a four to six inch layer of organic matter (leaves, compost, peat moss, shredded or chipped bark or wood—anything that has been alive) will help retain the moisture and improve your soil immeasurably as it breaks down.

A simple test will tell you if your drainage is poor: dig a small hole about the size of a gallon pot and fill with water. Wait for it to drain and fill again. If it takes over eight hours to drain, you need to make some changes to improve the drainage. The reason clay soil drains so slowly is because the water, once it gets in between the minute particles of clay, attaches itself and has a hard time getting out. Adding a lot of organic matter is the easiest way to open up the tiny spaces and improve drainage.

In the fall, we need to water differently as the days get shorter and nights cooler. Even when we have hot spells in late September and October, plants don't have the same high water demands as during the summer because they don't lose as much water. Teaser rains can be deceptive at the end of a dry summer, so monitor carefully to be sure plants are receiving adequate water. You can use the finger test—stick your finger in the soil and feel for moisture a couple of inches down, or dig a hole six to ten inches deep and scoop and squeeze the soil with your hand. If it crumbles, add water.

As a general rule, do not turn dry clay in the summer or wet clay in the winter as you may create clods that can take years to correct. There are several schools of thought on tilling, but if you feel it's necessary, till only when a handful of clay soil crumbles easily in your hand.

Why Should I Mulch?

～

BY JULIE CARTER, JAN SPECHT AND KATHY REIFFENSTEIN

Mulch is any material applied to the soil surface in sufficient amount to have a beneficial effect on the soil. Almost anything you can spread over the soil will act as mulch. In the long run, you will save gardening time, decrease costs, suppress weed growth, and your plants will love you for it. Mulches can be organic, meaning they are rich in carbon-like compost or leaves or inorganic, like stones or plastic.

A major advantage of organic mulch is that it will improve the physical structure and permeability of the soil. In the Bay area, this means that instead of clay, the upper level of your soil will be that wonderful dark brown, loose, earthy-smelling soil that most plants love. The depth of that great soil naturally depends on how regularly you mulch. As the mulch slowly breaks down, it releases nutrients into the soil and if you mulch regularly, little or no additional fertilizer will be needed. Mulches such as wood chips, bark and grass clippings have a high carbon content and tend to bind nitrogen; thus, adding one pound of nitrogen per cubic yard will compensate for this temporary loss. These nutrients are not only available to the plants but are also the energy source for the beneficial soil microorganisms and earthworms that further contribute to good soil structure.

In addition to improving the soil, mulch will protect against erosion, which occurs when bare soil is hit by the force of water from sprinklers or rain. It also prevents mud from spattering up onto the plant, thereby avoiding certain fungal diseases.

Mulch conserves soil moisture by preventing the hot sun and wind from directly striking the soil and drying it out. This significantly reduces evaporation and therefore water use. Remember to decrease your watering times when you mulch. Mulch also insulates, limiting soil temperature fluctuation. In the summer, the roots stay as much as 10°F cooler if the proper amount of mulch is applied. This means plants require less water and there is less chance for them to become water-stressed. In winter, mulch can prevent the freezing-thawing cycle in the upper layers of the soil, which causes heaving of the soil resulting in damage to roots.

All gardeners hate the thankless task of weeding. When mulch is applied thickly enough (about three to five inches), it blocks out light so weed seeds (and all other seeds) cannot germinate. If a few do manage to germinate, they are usually weaker and easier to pull out. Proper mulching will dramatically reduce weeds, resulting in less work to do and hopefully eliminating the need for using "weed killer" poisons (herbicides). However, do not try to smother established weeds. They are usually quite strong and many will grow through the mulch. It is best to pull them out with the roots or at the very least, cut at ground level before applying mulch.

Mulch can also enhance the aesthetic look of the garden. It is an attractive and beneficial carpet for the soil and can showcase the plants to maximum advantage. One can customize the look of the garden depending on the type of mulch chosen. And because the carpet is so pleasing to look at, no one has to plant excessively in an attempt to hide the bare soil or the drip irrigation lines.

It is even possible to mulch on a hillside. This is a situation where the type of mulch matters because you don't want it rolling off the hill! The shredded types of bark work well here. Because they are tangled, they hold together and, when damp or wet, cling to the soil. Container plants also love to be mulched.

Despite the many benefits of mulching, there can be some minor problems. Although mulches work well to control weeds, some mulches like hay, straw and fresh manure often contain weed seeds and may make your weed problem worse. Some mulches may be a fire hazard. Hay, straw, pine needles and peat moss are more highly flammable than others. When organic mulch is not completely composted, it can become "sour", containing methane, alcohol and other toxic gases that harm plants. Symptoms such as yellow or scorched leaves, defoliation or death of the plant may occur. However, none of these issues should prevent you from applying mulch. The benefits far outweigh the risks. Choosing the right kind of mulch for your garden and applying it properly can decrease or eliminate these problems.

Choosing the Right Mulch

Most mulches, whether organic or inorganic, are common, ordinary materials. The most popular organic mulches are compost, grass clippings, pine needles, sawdust and shredded leaves or bark. Popular inorganic mulches are plastic (clear and black), chips of marble and rocks. The best type for you depends largely on what's available and how much area you need to cover. Do remember that organic mulches improve the soil and give you a healthier garden, while inorganic ones do not. Some of your choices are:

- Peat moss decomposes slowly and has a reliable pH (3.4 to 4.8) acidity; it is good to add to our typically heavy, high pH soils. Peat moss is particularly beneficial around azaleas, rhododendrons and conifers since these plants require a more acidic soil.
- Decorative bark chips are usually a fairly uniform size. They are readily available in bags from garden centers. Bark chips are light to reddish brown in color, durable, easy to spread, slow to decompose and quite attractive. Spread coarse bark chips in a thicker layer than you would other materials—three to six inches—if you want to effectively conserve water. Small chips are more likely to blow away; large ones are more wind resistant. All turn gray with age.
- Shredded bark has a natural look and decomposes very slowly. The pieces are not uniform in size and therefore hold well on slopes and in windy areas. Apply at least two inches deep.
- Leaves tend to pack together when whole, so they are more effective if they're shredded with a shredder or a lawn mower.

~ Soil, Its Composition and Health ~

Leaves tend to decompose fairly quickly and may have to be replenished more than once a year.
- Wood chips are the result of hardwood branches put through a machine that chops them into chips. Check with local tree service companies who may gladly deliver them free of charge to your house. Apply at least two inches deep.
- Pine needles are slow to decay and therefore don't need frequent replenishment; they can, however, be a fire hazard. They should be applied at least six inches deep.
- Lawn clippings make a very effective mulch, but make sure your lawn is free of weeds such as crabgrass and Bermuda grass. Dry the clippings for a day or so in thin layers on pavement or plastic before using as mulch, or they will cake and breed flies.
- Compost can be homemade (the stuff you make yourself from garden clippings and fruit and vegetable leftovers) or commercial (the stuff you purchase in a bag from your nursery or home center). Before you spread homemade compost, sift it to remove any large, uncomposted pieces.
- Rice hulls are soft, very absorbent, and are found as an ingredient in many commercial mixes. Because of their lightness, you may want to cover them with a thin layer of heavier mulch, so they don't blow around. Apply them two to four inches deep.
- Straw and hay can be purchased at feed stores. Pull off four-inch thick layers from the bale and place them around plants or between rows without breaking apart. Straw has the advantage of containing very little seed, whereas hay contains a lot. This seed will germinate into weeds. When hayseed germinates, you can turn the layers over to get rid of emerging plants. These mulches can attract insects, slugs and snails. They are also flammable.
- Nut hulls should be applied two to three inches deep. This mulch generally lasts up to two years and can have an attractive appearance. Uncrushed shells are slow to decompose, although oily shells decompose more quickly. The sharp

edges of the shells may inhibit earthworm activity. Peanut hulls are not recommended as they can contain nematodes.
- Cocoa bean hulls are attractive and fragrant and have a measurable amount of nitrogen, yet are low in acidity. Imported hulls are not recommended as they can contain pesticide residues.

Inorganic mulches, normally plastics or rock, do not break down and therefore are considered to be more permanent than organic mulches. They raise the temperature of the soil and will benefit heat-loving plants most. Clear plastic will raise soil temperature faster than black plastic and allows some weeds to sprout under it; black plastic kills all weeds. Whenever using plastics, always water the ground before laying them down.

Rocks of varying size make good mulches and come in many colors and shades, that can add to a garden's good looks. Some gardeners put plastic underneath the rocks to stop weeds from sprouting. If chosen correctly, the rocks will retain moisture in the soil, yet allow rainwater to penetrate easily. Some popular inorganic mulches are:

- Stone and rock have interesting textures and shapes. They can be difficult to deal with in borders or raised beds and loose rocks can become a problem along pathways.
- Black plastic is non-degradable. It is very moisture retentive and warms the soil, thereby speeding maturity and increased yields of heat-loving plants. It suppresses most weeds since it is not air or water permeable.
- White plastic is the same as black, although it can allow more weeds to grow. It can cool the soil and intensify the light around the plant.
- Perforated or porous plastic has the same characteristics as the other plastic mulches, but water and air can penetrate.
- Landscape fabric is very durable and can be found at most nurseries or home centers. It is air and water permeable and preserves the life of the mulch directly under it. It suppresses

~ *Soil, Its Composition and Health* ~

most weeds below the mulch, although grass-like weeds can still penetrate.

How and When to Mulch

Mulching is one of the easiest gardening activities you can do. Once you've chosen your mulch material and have it in the area where you want to mulch, simply pour or scoop the mulch into piles between plants. Then, using your hands or a trowel, spread it to cover the area. Some mulches are tilled into the soil before planting to improve soil fertility and chemistry.

How deeply you should mulch depends on the material you're using. Loose mulches made up of large particles should be spread more thickly than finer mulches. As a rule of thumb, spread one to two inches of sawdust, two to three inches of coarser materials such as bark, four to six inches of loose hay, up to six inches of pine needles.

Be careful not to mulch too thickly or you will make it impossible for water and oxygen to reach the plant roots. You'll also create a cool, moist hiding place for mice, voles and other rodents that feed on plant stems and roots. Don't pack the mulch right up against the plant stems as this can encourage the development of diseases.

It's best to spread mulch in the fall so it can start to break down before spring planting; an application in the fall will help protect plants from any winter freeze. However, mulch can also be applied successfully in spring or summer, when it will help to conserve water and retain moisture in the soil. Your mulch will likely need to be replenished each year, depending on the type and how thickly you originally applied it.

Your rewards for mulching will be many. The best one is that your garden will be healthier. Healthy plants resist diseases best so there will be less need for pesticides and herbicides, and that will directly benefit our Bay area bays and creeks. And your gardening work, as well as cost, will be decreased.

Creating Compost — Garden Magic

by Diane Lynch

There is no better way to improve the Bay area's heavy clay soils than to add organic matter: turn it into your soil or mulch, mulch, mulch. One of the easiest ways to do it is to make your own in the form of compost. It's the ultimate way to recycle garden and kitchen waste and cut down your contributions to the landfill.

Making compost is actually a very simple process that takes place naturally in any forest on a continuing basis. Just look under the leaf and branch accumulation in a forest to see finished compost: black, crumbly, earthy-looking material. As you contemplate making compost for your garden, answer these questions.

Are you a casual gardener with little time and not a lot of energy to devote to the garden? You may want to use a slower "pile it and leave it" technique that will yield compost after six or more months.

Are you an ambitious gardener with a lot of time to spend in the garden and a high level of energy? You could consider making "hot" compost that can be accomplished in as little as three weeks. The rapid "hot" compost technique developed by the University of California's Clarence Golueke relies on small particle size and frequent turning to keep the pile very hot, speeding decomposition.

The first things to consider in making compost are: where and in what? A utility area out of your primary view of the garden, near a water hose, would be best. Garden trimmings can simply be piled on the ground but it will be neater and faster if you make a bottomless container that will hold about a cubic yard, three feet by three feet by three feet. Just about anything that will allow some air to enter can be used for the sides: old lumber, window screens or other wire mesh, forklift pallets—look around with a creative eye. An ideal setup would have three piles so you have a new pile, a working pile and a pile that is finishing. If you live on a hillside you can make the hill contribute some of the labor if you build three piles, each above the other so they stair step down the hill. When you want to turn one, simply remove the partition and rake the compost down into the next bin.

Cold Compost

To make cold or passive compost:
Simply fill the bin as the material accumulates and allow it to sit until decomposed. The chemical composition of hot and cold compost varies and some research has indicated that slowly-produced compost may actually have disease-resisting capabilities that the hot kind does not. It takes a lot more time and garden space to make it the slow way.

Hot Compost

To make hot or fast compost:

- Have equal parts brown (carbon source: dried leaves, woody garden trimmings, straw, sawdust, even shredded newspaper) and green (nitrogen source: freshly-cut garden trimmings, food scraps, grass clippings) material, enough to fill your pile or bin all at once. You can stockpile brown materials and use them to build a pile when you have large quantities of moist greens, which do not store well.
- Put some coarse material (sticks, straw, a forklift pallet) as a base to provide air under the pile.
- Chop, shred or mow green and brown materials to make small particles under one-half inch in size. Mix brown and green together, adding enough water as you put it in the bin so that it is moist, about the consistency of a wrung-out sponge. Don't press down contents: the process relies on adequate moisture and oxygen to get and keep decomposing organisms living in the pile. Commercial compost "starters" aren't necessary—you already have plenty of microorganisms.

- The center of the pile will heat up rapidly to as much as 160°F. You can buy a compost thermometer at a garden supply and you will know it's time to turn the pile when the temperature starts to drop, in two to four days. Strive to keep the middle of the pile about 140°F. In the absence of a thermometer, put your fist about a foot into the center of the pile—it should be uncomfortably warm. When turning, use a thin-tined fork to pitch the contents into the next bin, working the sides into the center where the microorganisms do the fastest decomposing.
- A cover will slow the evaporation of water in warm dry weather and keep out excessive rain in the winter which can leach nutrients as well as create an anaerobic, unproductive compost pile. Covers can be made from straw or solid material such as wood or a tarp.

What Not to Compost

Do not compost meat products, grease, oils, bones, manure from meat eaters (such as dogs, cats, humans), charcoal ashes, weeds with seeds that may not break down or noxious weeds such as poison oak, broom.

Problems?

If your compost pile

- has an unpleasant ammonia odor, nitrogen level is too high: correct by adding more brown or carbon ingredients such as straw, leaves, sawdust when turning the pile.
- doesn't heat up within a couple of days, it could be too wet or too dry: correct an overly wet condition by adding more brown material when turning; if it appears too dry, add water while turning.
- doesn't heat up but moisture seems about right: add some high nitrogen material such as fresh grass clippings, blood meal or cottonseed meal while turning.
- attracts flies, rats and other neighborhood critters: food may have been added to top of the pile and not securely covered.

It should be buried in the center, under about twelve inches of garden matter. A little wood ash sprinkled on top tends to deter these pests. If rodents continue to be a problem, it's best to keep food scraps out of the pile or to build a bin of wire mesh.

More Thoughts

Consider these potential refinements to your compost pile:

- A piece of PVC pipe drilled at close, random intervals standing vertically in the center of the pile can be jiggled to add oxygen.
- Leaves can be chopped in a garbage can with a string trimmer, mowed with a lawn mower equipped with a leaf bag, or shredded in a shredder.
- Alternate composting containers include plastic bags (punch air holes in bags of leaves, add a little water, set aside to decompose); trash can with no bottom, holes drilled in sides; commercially purchased or homemade barrels on a stand that can be rotated to speed the process and cut the labor of turning.

Garden Magic

The benefits of mulching with compost are many. Compost mulch:

- retains water in the soil in summer heat
- insulates plant roots in summer and winter
- boosts levels of microorganisms as well as earthworms in soil
- improves texture and ability to work the soil
- provides a slow-release fertilizer to plants

When using compost as a mulch, just top dress plants with a two to six inch layer or mix it into the soil when replanting annuals or between perennials. There's no need to dig it in—the earthworms that will abound in your garden will do the work for you, as well as aerating the soil and enriching it with their castings.

HMO for Healthy Soil

by Jan Specht

Healthy soil requires organic matter and beneficial soil organisms to decompose the organic matter, thereby creating nutrients for plants. Fertilizers only provide nutrients and do nothing to help the soil.

Plants require seventeen nutrient elements. Carbon, hydrogen and oxygen are in air and water. The primary nutrients are nitrogen (N), phosphorus (P), and potassium (K, also called potash) and are seen on fertilizer labels as NPK, and always in that order. They are called primary because they are used in larger quantities than other nutrients, not because they are more important. In Bay area soils, nitrogen is usually the most deficient nutrient. Phosphorus and potassium are present in soil, but phosphorus is bound in compounds that are relatively insoluble in water and potassium is combined with minerals that plants can't use. These three nutrients are most often the limiting factors in growing plants. Secondary nutrients are calcium, magnesium and sulfur. In commercial fertilizers, primary and secondary nutrients are measured as a percent of their dry weight. For example, NPK 5-5-5 in a ten-pound bag means there is 5% of ten pounds, or one-half pound, of each nutrient in that package.

Micronutrients are measured as parts per million (ppm) of dry weight and include iron, boron, zinc, manganese, chlorine, copper, nickel and molybdenum. It is best to use the term micronutrients to refer to mineral elements that are essential for plant growth in trace amounts. However, sometimes the terms trace elements, microelements, heavy metals, trace metals, or trace inorganics are used interchangeably with micronutrients. Sometimes other elements are listed as micronutrients even though they have no known physiologic function.

Fertilizers

Complete fertilizers contain nitrogen, phosphorus and potassium, but may or may not contain other nutrients. Complete fertilizers may be formulated for a specific plant such as roses or tomatoes. Sometimes, but not always, custom fertilizer combinations are based on field research trials so the proportions of nutrients are optimal for that plant.

A soil analysis can be done to identify deficiencies, but home test kits are not very accurate and laboratory tests can be expensive depending on the number of items to be tested. The typical tests are for nitrogen, phosphorus and potassium. Checking for micronutrients usually is not necessary. Only rarely will a home garden need a soil analysis. The first signs of inadequate amounts of nitrogen, phosphorus, potassium, magnesium or molybdenum are seen in older leaves because these elements are mobile and can move out of older leaves into younger ones. Early deficiencies of calcium, sulfur, iron, copper, zinc or manganese show up in young leaves first because these elements are immobile.

Soil Amendments

Soil amendments are not the same as fertilizers. Strictly speaking, amendments promote plant growth indirectly. One way is by altering the acidity or alkalinity of soil. If soil is too acidic, it can be amended with lime, and if too alkaline, sulfur can be added. The pH (potential Hydrogen) scale ranges from 0 to 14. Numbers below 7 are in the acid range, over 7 are in the alkaline range and seven is neutral. The pH is important because some soil nutrients are available to plants in acid soil, most are available in neutral soil and some are absorbed best in alkaline soil. Rhododendrons and azaleas require an acid soil and will show signs of iron deficiency, even in the presence of iron, if the soil pH is too high. Lowering the pH appropriately will allow adequate iron uptake.

Amendments can also promote growth by changing the physical structure of soil. When adequate amounts of organic matter are added to clay soil, the eventual result is a loose, dark soil with a structure very different from clay. Organic matter can therefore act both as an amendment by changing soil structure and as a fertilizer because soil organisms decompose the organic matter and release nutrients.

As helpful as fertilizers seem to be, they do nothing to improve soil. In some agricultural fields it is possible to find non-decomposed cornstalks, thatch and other plant waste that was plowed under one or two seasons earlier because beneficial soil organisms are absent. Home gardens that rely only on fertilizers also have soils that are depleted. When soil structure declines, water holding capacity decreases and more fertilizer leaches through the soil. Leaching and runoff remove large amounts of nutrients so fewer plants will grow, increasing the risk of soil erosion. This leads to applying increasing amounts of fertilizers, which cause excess nitrogen and salts in the soil. Fast acting fertilizers including animal manures tend to be high in salts. Excess salts and nitrogen leach into the subsoil with the risk of contaminating ground water and of being carried in runoff into our creeks and Bay. Excess salts also repel earthworms. Excess nitrogen can 'burn' plant leaves by drawing water out of root cells causing them to dehydrate. The plant, or parts of it, appears brown and extremely dry giving it a 'burned' look. Excess fertilization produces lush growth, which predisposes the plant to disease problems, especially aphids. Sometimes the tendency is to use more fertilizer than the package recommends in hopes of not having to apply it as often. Because most fertilizers release their nutrients faster than plants can use them, it is better to apply less at a time and apply it more often so it is less likely to end up in ground water or runoff. Slow-release fertilizers are less of a problem when used in appropriate amounts. Slow-release means nutrients are more consistently available in smaller quantities so plants are able to use at least ninety percent of them.

Soil Organic Matter

Soil organic matter has other benefits in addition to improving soil structure and contributing to plant nutrients. It improves water retention while also improving drainage and aeration. Healthy soil is

~ *Soil, Its Composition and Health* ~

an ecosystem that is constantly changing. It contains a large variety and huge number of beneficial microorganisms (fungi, bacteria, algae and others) as well as larger organisms such as earthworms. One would expect healthy soil to produce healthier plants and research has shown that beneficial soil microbes can help control some plant diseases, especially root pathogens. The actual composition of soil varies depending on the source of the organic matter.

The easiest way to add organic matter to garden soil is to use compost. It can be purchased or made free at home from yard and kitchen plant waste. Research shows it is possible to meet the nutrient requirements of most plants by applying compost regularly. Because compost releases nutrients slowly, over time there will be ample nutrients stored in soil. Home compost made from grass, leaves and plant kitchen waste releases about fifteen percent of its nitrogen the first season. The eighty five percent is stored in soil and released gradually. When growing edible crops, every one hundred square feet uses about one-third pound of nitrogen per season. If backyard compost is used, a layer of slightly less than one inch provides this amount. Compare this to adding three to four inches of compost twice a year as mulch (the usual recommendation) and it is easy to see why additional nitrogen is not necessary after the first year if the soil has been amended in the past. If only commercial fertilizers have been used and the soil has never been amended, it will take a few years to built soil fertility, but improvement will be seen after the first year. Supplemental nitrogen can be applied in decreasing amounts as the transition progresses.

The nitrogen, phosphorus and potassium in organic fertilizers seem quite low compared to amounts in most synthetic fertilizers. But because they are stored in soil, slowly released and applied in greater volume (mulch), that is plenty. Other benefits of mulch are prevention of weed seed germination, erosion control, protection of roots from temperature extremes and decreased water use. It is possible to over fertilize even with organic products and damage soil life, predispose plants to pest problems and pollute water, so don't exceed recommended amounts.

Diagnosing Common Disorders

by Kathy Reiffenstein

Sickly, yellowish foliage on your favorite plant may have you running for the pesticide spray, convinced that a new pest has invaded your garden. But think again. Such yellowing may not be a pest or disease, but rather a problem caused by adverse environmental conditions. These abiotic (non-living or non-infectious) disorders can be caused by numerous things, including air pollution, too few or too many nutrients, too much or too little water, pesticides, too much or not enough sun, and frost. These disorders not only inflict their own damage on a plant, they also weaken it and make the plant more susceptible to attack by pests and diseases.

Discolored, distorted or dying foliage is the typical sign of an abiotic disorder, although damage from insects, fungi, bacteria and viruses can also produce similar symptoms. Before deciding how to treat the problem, it's important to decide what's causing the damage.

Providing plants with the appropriate amount of water is always a challenge. Although the outward symptoms of both too little and too much water can be similar, over watering is usually a more common problem. If there is too much water in the soil, it prevents oxygen from getting to the plant's roots, thereby smothering them. As roots die, the foliage above ground starts to discolor and die. Over watering also promotes fungal root diseases such as *Armillaria*.

Under watering will cause leaves to wilt, fade in color to a dull shade, and drop prematurely. The new growth at the tips of the plant may wilt in the afternoon and then recover in the evening. If the plant is under prolonged stress, due to lack of water, new leaves will be smaller and the plant will become increasingly susceptible to insects and disease. Examine your plants regularly and carefully for signs of water inadequacy or excess, and adjust your watering.

~ Soil, Its Composition and Health ~

Water lawns and gardens in the early morning (even just before dawn) to minimize water loss from evaporation. Foliage will dry quickly at this time of the day, and therefore be less susceptible to the development of foliar diseases such as leaf spot and rust.

Mineral deficiencies also cause leaves to yellow and fade. If a plant is lacking iron, the new foliage will be small and it will fade to a yellowish green, starting at the edges of the leaf and spreading inward until only the veins remain green. Often an element other than iron is lacking or if, for example, the camellia suffers from soil compaction, both may look like iron deficiency. If the plant is lacking nitrogen, the entire older leaves will uniformly turn yellow.

To correct iron-deficient soil, aerate the soil around the roots and spread an iron chelate evenly over the soil beneath the plant canopy or apply it to the foliage, according to the product label. If you regularly mulch with composted organic matter, you will eventually remedy the iron deficiency. Some soils in the Bay area are stubbornly alkaline. In such cases, apply finely ground agricultural sulfur. Sulfur should not be used at temperatures above 80°F because it becomes toxic to plants. Spread sulfur as broadly as conditions in your garden allow.

A nitrogen deficiency can be fixed quickly by applying a nitrate fertilizer. However, this will tend to promote rapid, succulent growth, which attracts aphids and mites. Another choice is an organic form of nitrogen, such as compost, which must decompose before being absorbed by plants, thus preventing excessive foliage growth.

Sunburn is another abiotic hazard. Sunburn shows up in the areas between the veins of the foliage, appearing as a yellow or brown area, and then the foliage begins to die in that area. Specifically, vegetation growing in compacted soil is prone to sunburn. A combination of too much light and heat and not enough moisture is what causes sunburn. Choose plants that are well suited to the site where they're being planted–that is, don't plant a shade-loving plant in bright, full sun. Monitor plants for signs of sunburn. Aerate their roots before providing adequate water.

CHAPTER FOUR

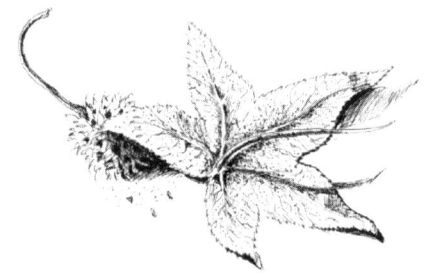

Seasonal Gardening

Plant Some Spring Happiness!

by Stacy Nelson

"He who plants a garden, plants happiness" says an ancient Chinese proverb. As an avid aspiring gardener, I plant a lot of happiness in spring. Officially spring begins March 20th. Our last Bay area frost is roughly March 15th. Any time after that is right to visit local nurseries, dust off garden tools and begin spring plantings.

Plant Seedlings

In January and February we spend most of our time planning the structure of our garden and possibly doing some pruning. In February and early March, we start seedlings indoors. At the end of March we may begin to plant those seedlings. Begin when the rains have stopped as seedlings can experience damping-off if too moist.

Summer Bulbs

Summer bulbs like dahlias, which are great for cutting, begonias, gladiolus (choose high-crowned corms) and lilies can be planted in spring. Plant spring and summer annuals and perennials like coreopsis, coneflower, gloriosa daisy, yarrow and statice.

Vegetables

Finish planting cool season vegetables, which grow best at average temperatures of 55°F to 75°F. March is the time to finish planting radishes, onion bulbs, peas and potatoes if you did not already do so in February. Set out broccoli, celery and lettuce. Sow seeds of summer vegetables and annuals indoors.

Pair Plantings for Healthier Results

Consider planting certain plants, believed to provide protection against pests, next to those more vulnerable. Early American colonists learned this trick from the native Indians and it is still popular today. Planting petunias near beans keeps away bean beetles. Garlic and onions near roses prevent black spot, mildew and aphids. Nasturtiums' edible blooms dress up salads and deter squash bugs. Thyme deters cabbageworms. Make your tomatoes taste better by planting basil next to them. Calendula, or marigolds, are also good for general garden ailments if you don't mind their pungent scent. Marigolds lure potato beetles away from potatoes and deter nematodes. Coreopsis is a good insect controller for neighboring plants. Tall perennial flowers can help shade lettuce. Onions repel rabbits. Daffodil bulbs, which are planted in the fall, are said to deter burrowing animals such as moles. The list goes on and on. The key is to incorporate complementary planting and keep your garden healthy.

Is the Grass Greener on the Other Side of the Fence?

Determine what has already grown successfully in your area. Palm trees and artichokes may not make it in your garden. Look to the natural environment. Oak trees, bays and ceanothus landscapes will find more success with native drought resistant plants. If you live near a creek or redwoods and experience more fog in the morning, plant an area with rhizomes that thrive with additional water. Stroll through your neighborhood and eye your neighbors' plantings. What is growing well in their gardens?

Don't be discouraged if you have planted new shrubs and perennials in the last couple of years and they don't seem to be growing very much. There is a rule of thumb that says it takes three years to fully establish new plantings.

Consider the different microclimates within your own backyard. Is there a spot that gets more wind or more sun? Remember the southeast corner of your garden gets the most sun and therefore may be the best spot for your roses or your vegetables. Work with nature, not against it, and use only plants that will thrive in your area.

Summer Pruning Slows Overgrown Fruit Trees

by Diane Lynch

It is usually recommended that fruit trees be pruned at the end of winter into very early spring, with the objective of increasing exposure of the fruits and leaves to light. This is the dormant season for fruit trees — the time after the leaves drop and before the buds begin to swell in early spring. Dormant pruning stimulates shoot growth, reduces the number of fruits, and increases fruit size.

But give some consideration to pruning mature fruit trees during the growing season — there are some specific benefits, and for certain trees, it can be the best time to prune. The dwarf and semi-dwarf rootstocks commonly used for fruit trees do not control tree size as much as people might expect, so summer pruning can be a useful tool for keeping tree size manageable. Summer pruning increases light intensity, improves fruit color and stimulates flower buds. Do not, however, summer prune young trees in the first four years of development.

Studies have shown that summer pruning has a dwarfing effect, decreasing shoot growth, which over time reduces the overall size of a tree. Since the leaves are the food factory for the tree, when you remove branches you remove food-producing portions of the tree which results in reduced output and size of the plant; food storage is also reduced over the coming winter, which controls vigor the following spring. With dormant pruning, the energy reserve is left unchanged, since energy is stored mostly in the trunk and root system during fall and winter. Because spring growth is so vigorous, early pruning produces more growth than pruning done later in spring or summer.

Early summer pruning in June and July has the greatest potential to dwarf the tree and should be used to limit the upright water sprouts and current season's vigorous growth. Only thinning cuts should be used. A thinning cut takes a branch back to the next branch as opposed to a heading cut that snips off growth to a bud and stimulates many small branches to form. Since fruit trees ideally should be kept to a height where one can handpick the fruit from the ground or on a small stool, summer pruning is a good way to keep an overly vigorous tree under control. Pruning at this time is the best way to reduce vegetative growth and prevent shoot development. Plum trees in particular can be so out of control that summer can be the best time of year to prune them, but this applies to any fruit tree that needs to be reined in. Be aware that the root system and eventually, the whole tree, is also dwarfed by early summer pruning, so it may be best not to summer prune every year. Rather, use summer pruning as a selective technique along with yearly dormant pruning.

Midsummer pruning in July and August stimulates little vegetative growth and is less likely to dwarf the root system as compared to early summer pruning. This can be a good time to reduce the height and width of trees by trimming back new growth. The amount to remove depends on the age, growth and vigor of the tree, but a tree with a good crop could have the new growth reduced by half to two-thirds. This will have the effect of letting in more sunlight to color the fruit and reduce vegetative growth, making more sugars available to the maturing fruit and potentially resulting in improved flavor. Two possible downsides are reduced fruit size and the potential for sunburned fruit and foliage. Summer pruning is necessary to keep espaliered and formally trained trees under control and properly disciplined. Cease pruning a couple of months prior to your average fall frost date to prevent winter damage to trees.

If you have overgrown trees that have not been pruned for years, it is best to rejuvenate them over a period of three years. Very heavy pruning should be avoided whenever possible as it exposes internal branches to sunscald, increasing the likelihood of attack by borers and

~ *Seasonal Gardening* ~

fungi, and it upsets the fruiting process. New growth will occur in areas that are pruned, so prune thinner areas to stimulate growth and thin fuller areas minimally. Regular light to moderate pruning is the best way to keep trees in good condition.

General rules for pruning mature fruit trees:

- prune to leave horizontal branches, thinning out those growing up or down
- remove dead, diseased or broken wood any time of year
- make close, neat cuts almost flush with the adjacent branch, just outside the wrinkly "collar"—stubs encourage disease and heal slowly
- prune moderately and regularly—heavy pruning should be avoided
- eliminate the less desirable of two crossing branches, attempting to keep the more horizontal branch
- angle cuts so they shed water to discourage rot

Pruning is an art as well as a science and there are multiple acceptable ways to prune any tree. Attend a pruning class at your local nursery or one offered by Master Gardeners and then get out there and learn to prune by pruning; observe the results over time to improve your technique.

November Is Time to Plant

~

BY MAGGIE AGRO

If you want a positively stunning garden next spring, November is the time to plant for dramatic results. Planted in November, cool-season annuals and perennials develop a strong root system that will allow an early show in April or May.

If using annuals, set out forget-me-nots, Iceland poppies, ornamental cabbage and kale, pansies, snapdragons, and sweet alyssum. It's too late to use six-packs, so set out four-inch pots.

For perennials, look for artemesia, campanula, coral bells, lamium, penstemon, phlox, salvia, and Oriental poppies. If the perennials in your garden had smaller blooms this year or seemed overly crowded, autumn is the time to divide them. Plants suitable for dividing include: asters, bellflowers, callas, daisies, and daylilies. Gently pull or dig up overgrown clumps, leaving root balls intact. Pull gently while washing, either in a pail of water or under a gentle spray. Each newly divided clump should have both leaves and roots. Add organic matter to the soil and replant the divisions immediately. Some perennials with stronger roots, such as agapanthus or daylilies, may require use of a spading fork.

November is also a time to set out cold hardy ground covers, shrubs, trees and vines. Any kind of a plant that is not frost tender can get off to a fast start in the cool months ahead. Plant shrubs with multi-seasonal appeal like cotoneaster and pyracantha that provide flowers in the spring followed by deep colored berries.

Buy spring-blooming bulbs by choosing those that are firm and haven't started sprouting. Plant daffodils, irises, tulips and daylilies. Chill crocus and hyacinths in the refrigerator in paper bags before planting, being careful not to store with apples or fruit that produces

~ Seasonal Gardening ~

ethylene gas. Plant bulbs in two or three layers that bloom sequentially, or over plant with pansies or Iceland poppies for color while you wait. Planting charts with information on when and how long bulbs bloom and how deep to plant are available at your nursery.

Bulbs are graded for size, just like eggs. Usually, the bigger the circumference, the more flowers you get. When you are planting a large quantity, it makes most sense to choose mid-size bulbs. And beware of promotions that sell a large quantity of bulbs for a really cheap price. You may end up with bulbs that produce very few flowers. Find out from catalogs how bulbs are graded and buy accordingly.

Some bulbs can be classified as naturalizers. These are the bulbs that behave as perennials and come back every year, even multiplying. They are relatively pest free and easy to plant. You can just toss these bulbs onto the earth, cover with two to four inches of soil and mulch and forget them. They include bluebells, callas, daffodils, freesias, grape hyacinth, bearded iris, Dutch iris, Asian and Oriental lilies. Avoid tiger lilies, which carry diseases that affect other bulbs.

For natural protection from pests as well as a show of color, sow native wildflower mixes to attract butterflies and beneficial insects or select mixes for color or fragrance. Be thorough in removing weeds from your planting space or you will have a bumper crop growing through your wildflowers.

Winter vegetables can be set out now, including seedlings of broccoli, cabbage, cauliflower, lettuce and spinach. While shopping for veggies at the nursery, pick up several purple and magenta ornamental kales. To brighten your spirits with a burst of color when winter turns dreary, plant these annuals in a gray galvanized pail or weathered basket for a stunning show. Sow seeds of beets, carrots, leeks, onions, peas, radishes, and turnips. Plant garlic cloves in full sun and well drained soil about two inches deep.

No matter what you plant, remember to water if the rainfall is sporadic or very light. Cool, dry winds can dry out the soil. Mix in a controlled release fertilizer at planting time to avoid the need for additional feeding during the first season.

Plant California Native Bulbs This Fall

by Barbara J. Euser

Fragile fairy lanterns, pale purple brodiaea, creamy mariposa lilies—all are California natives which grow from bulbs. These and other natives display delicate hues and complex forms. They are naturally perfectly suited to the local climate. Many are drought tolerant, although some prefer a damp spot in the garden.

Flowers synonymous with spring—iris, tulips, trillium—propagate by division of underground structures. Bulbs are modified leaf bases enclosing buds. Corms and rhizomes are thickened stems.

Earliest in the spring, trillium bloom. As their name suggests, their leaves grow in a three-leafed whorl, topped by a maroon or white flower with three petals. They prefer a shady part of the garden and are comfortable among ferns and azaleas. Growing from a single rhizome, trillium will slowly increase into a clump.

Mid-spring, iris show their colors. Eleven species of Pacific Coast iris form their own group within the iris genus. California native iris reputedly spread through creeping rhizomes to form clumps that can be divided during wet winter months. Although the Douglas iris, *Iris douglasiana*, I planted in my garden have not spread much, I trust they will live up to their reputation. Douglas iris range from pale to dark purple in color. Other forms of iris have been crossed with this species to produce Pacific Coast Hybrids, or PCH. They cover a broad palette of colors, from copper to pink, bright yellow to maroon.

Fairy lanterns bloom beginning in March. The white fairy lantern or globe tulip, *Calochortus albus*, is widespread in woodlands from San Francisco Bay south through the Sierra foothills. The golden globe tulip, *C. amabilis*, is more compact and has rich yellow blooms. The *Calochortus* genus also includes the mariposa lily, of which there are at least a dozen species of California natives. They range in habitat from grasslands to chaparral, from coastal foothills to low deserts.

Another genus with a number of native California species is Brodiaea, or harvest lily. These grow from corms in a variety of soils, from heavy adobe to mountain meadows. During the summer, they need to rest and therefore require no water. Brodiaea flowers are a cluster of glossy blue or purple funnels at the top of a stem. There are low-growing brodiaea such as *B. nana* with pale blue flowers that tolerates adobe soil. Other brodiaea grow tall: stately *B. californica* shows purple blooms from May to July.

Plants which used to be considered Brodiaea have now been separated into their own genus. These close relatives include the wild hyacinth and blue dicks, now called Dichelostemmas, and Ithuriel's Spear and Milk Lily, now called Triteleias. Dichelostemmas include the firecracker flower, *D. ida-maia*, an eye-catching cluster of red and green flowers which may grow up to three feet high. Others are blue dicks, *D. capitatum* and the wild hyacinth, *D. multiflorum*. All grow well in mixed bulb borders. Ithuriel's Spear, *Triteleia laxa*, is the most common and easiest to grow. Its purple flowers burst from stiff, leafless two-foot stalks.

California has many native lilies. They fall into two groups: those with creeping rhizomatous bulbs that require moisture year round and those with large single bulbs that need a dry summer to rest. The leopard lily, *Lilium pardalinum*, has orange or red-orange flowers with brown spots in a graceful, recurved form. It requires sufficient water year round. In its native habitat, it is widespread along streams and in wet meadows. One of the easiest native lilies to grow in the garden, over time leopard lilies will naturalize and form colonies. By contrast, the Humboldt lily, *L. humboldtii*, requires only occasional summer water. It has a similar spotted pattern on yellow-orange petals and blooms midsummer.

These are just some of the native California plants that grow from bulbs, corms and rhizomes. Fall is the best season to plant them as bulbs, although as plants from nurseries, they may be planted at other times of year. Rely on nurseries to provide plants or bulbs from ethical sources, that is, grown for gardening, not robbed from the wild. A number of local nurseries carry some of these species in one-gallon or smaller containers.

Preparing the Garden for Winter

by Elizabeth Finley

Late October and November is a great time to groom perennials. While you're at it, take the time now to cultivate and amend the soil and your beds and borders will be all set to grow and bloom next spring.

The first order of business is pruning and shaping, starting with shrubs and small trees. Most plants get too big for our gardens, so trim dead branches and twigs, branches that grow into the center of the plant and branches that are not growing where you want them to, for example, over a path. For shrubs like nandinas and viburnums that produce a cluster of stems, cut unproductive trunks to ground level.

Fall is an excellent time to shear back hedges. Cut at an angle so the base will be slightly wider than the top. Mature hedges can take heavy pruning – down to one set of leaves of this year's growth. Don't prune trees and shrubs that flower in the spring, like camellias, quince, azaleas, deciduous magnolias, cherry and plum trees, because you'll cut off all next year's flowers. Wait until January and February to prune roses, Japanese maples and fruiting trees. Keep clippers away from tender subjects like fuchsias and bougainvillea that will stand up to frost better with last season's growth still on.

Trim spent flowers and stems on perennials, cut yellowing foliage and pull dead leaves from agapanthus, ferns and other fountain-shaped perennials. Use hand shears to cut back stems of floppy salvias, coreopsis and geraniums to the spot where you see new sprouts. Trim just above a node — the spot on the branch where a leaf is attached — because new growth will sprout there. With fine-stemmed Santa Barbara daisies and fast growing hardy geraniums, just grab a handful of stems and whack off to the desired level; new growth will sprout along the stems. Shrubby perennials like lavenders, santolinas and some salvias can be lightly pruned and shaped; don't remove more than fifty percent of the green matter and never cut back into bare wood.

Yank out spent annuals, and while you're at it, dig up tubers of summer flowering plants like dahlias and tuberous begonias that usually rot in our wet winter soils. They can be stored in a cool, dry spot in a pot with some soil.

The secret of great gardens is to amend the soil every year to increase its capacity to hold air, water and nutrients around the roots. The result is strong, healthy plants that resist disease and insect attacks. The best soil amendment is compost, ideally your own homemade variety. If your soil is sandy, add peat moss along with compost to improve the water-holding ability of the soil; if you've got clay, dig in fir bark or rice hulls to increase the air penetration of heavy soil.

As long as the ground is not sopping wet, spread a two to three inch layer of organic soil amendment on the soil and cultivate it in. Don't cultivate around plants like azaleas, camellias, rhododendrons and Japanese maples that have roots on the soil surface; just pick up fallen leaves and debris and add fresh mulch.

Now is the time to add fertilizers like cottonseed meal or alfalfa pellets that need the action of soil microorganisms over many months to make their nitrogen available to plants; add a helping of compost to make sure the microorganisms are present.

Finally, bed down the garden in a coverlet of mulch. This is one of the best things you can do for your garden. It helps plant roots to grow, worms to proliferate and aerate the soil, and lets billions of helpful microorganisms go to work for you. Almost any material can be used as mulch – compost, bark chips, fallen leaves, cocoa or rice hulls. Compost is most nutritious; fallen leaves are most available. Use a shovel to pour a two to four inch layer of mulch in the back of the bed and rake it forward. Make sure the mulch is four to six inches away from the trunk of any plants; any closer it will promote crown rot.

Putting Your Garden to Bed

by Diane Lynch

Since we don't have much of a dormant season during our short, mild winters, there isn't a whole lot of prep work to do for a long hard winter; however, there are many garden tasks that are best accomplished in the fall. For starters, fall is the time to divide and transplant spring blooming perennials such as iris, daffodils, lilies, gladiolus, daylilies, agapanthus. It's also a great time to plant perennials, shrubs and container trees. Wait until January to plant roses and fruit trees and you'll find bare root stock available.

In my garden, fall is the time to play musical plants. The oakleaf hydrangea that the deer have been dining on this summer will be moving inside the fenced area. The scented geranium that unexpectedly grew to six feet will have to move over by the fence so I can get down the path. The magnificent lime green and purple-blossomed salvia that threatened to take over the entire side yard when it grew six feet by six feet will have to be sacrificed in my tiny garden, but I've taken cuttings to share with friends who have larger spaces, so it will live on.

One of the first rules of gardening is to plant according to a plan and put in plants sized to the area available so you don't have to prune excessively. But some plants inevitably end up in the wrong places, either because one can't predict their eventual size, they grow larger than predicted, or were planted too densely. In any event, fall is the ideal time to transplant such plants. They will be in a semi-dormant state and able to put down roots in the moist soil of winter.

Cleaning up leaves and other organic debris in the garden in the fall is a good idea as a control measure for many insects and diseases. It also helps manage slugs and snails that favor moist organic material

~ *Seasonal Gardening* ~

as daytime hiding places. Slugs' main breeding time is the fall, so keeping them under control then may make for less damage the following spring. One way to keep the numbers down is to go on nocturnal missions with a flashlight and add the deceased warriors to the compost pile. Some people report success in rounding up large numbers of these guys by inverting half of a grapefruit peel and checking it frequently to destroy those in hiding. Bran makes good bait: place it around the garden in small piles and check regularly at night to dispatch your victims. Some people swear by using scratchy substances such as eggshells but there isn't much evidence that this works. Slugs and snails tend to occur less frequently in sandy soils, but this is probably because sandy soils drain quickly. The water-retentive nature of clay soils makes them more attractive. The first line of defense in dealing with these pests is to limit their habitat by eliminating hiding places.

Fall is a great time to plant biennial seeds, such as hollyhocks, some poppies and Canterbury bells, so that they will flower next year. A biennial takes two years to complete its life cycle. The first year it will grow leaves but not flower. The second year it will flower, set seed and complete its lifecycle. By planting biennials a few years in a row you will ensure a continuous display of these flowers.

Many California natives are best planted from seed in the fall. Remember to prepare the soil by loosening it a bit with a rake and then scatter the seed. It helps to mix small seed with a little sand to ensure even distribution. Be sure to tamp the seed securely into the soil as good contact is essential to germination. Keep the soil damp until the rains take over. To foil seed-eating birds, sprinkle a light covering of fine compost, hay or straw over the bed.

If you must have a lawn, knowing there is nothing you can plant that will use more water or require more maintenance, then fall is a good time to put it in. Sod will root readily in the winter rains. Seeding, a less expensive alternative, will allow you to establish a lush lawn over winter when you won't want to be out walking on it anyway. There are some new dwarf fescues that require less water than bluegrass or Bermuda grass. Lawns tend to be over fertilized, which causes them to grow faster so they need more water, and you get to spend more time mowing, edging and sweeping. No fertilizer is necessary over the winter months. Plus, excess fertilizer washes into our Bay, causing some algae to grow out of control, using up oxygen and carbon dioxide in the water. Then the algae starts to die off and decompose, using still more oxygen, leaving none for the Bay animals.

So, just when you thought you could settle down in your armchair, it's time to get out in the garden and divide, transplant, clean up and sow seed. In addition, you could prune fall blooming plants after they bloom and plant bulbs such as tulips and daffodils that have been pre-chilled for about six weeks. Not to mention the fact that you could put in a winter vegetable garden of cool weather edibles such as radishes, lettuce, peas, broccoli, cabbage, onions and beets. If you are lucky, we'll have good rains so you will be compelled to stay off clay soil for fear of compaction, and then you'll have an excuse to study the seed catalogues and read a garden book or two.

Winter: To Prune or Not to Prune

by Diane Lynch

There is both art and science involved in good pruning. A skillful pruner can make a plant look natural and beautiful, as well as heal in a quick and healthy fashion. Now, during our short dormant season, is the best time to prune many plants: fruit trees, roses, deciduous oaks and other trees. Some plants, however, bloom on old growth and winter pruning will prevent flowering next year. If in doubt don't prune.

Plants will naturally shed branches as new ones are grown and when we prune, we accelerate that growth process. The most basic reasons for pruning are the three Ds: dead, damaged, diseased parts of plants should be removed. Diseased parts should be discarded in the trash rather than left in the garden to minimize spreading disease. Other reasons to prune include directing or training a plant to the shape you desire or to ensure a strong framework, as well as to increase flowering and fruit yield.

When you prune a plant, you are telling it to grow, and by pruning properly, you can direct the growth so the plant flowers and fruits the way you want it to.

There are two basic pruning cuts: thinning, which takes a branch back to a larger or main branch; and heading, which takes small amounts off the tips back to a bud. Thinning cuts are generally best. They open a plant to better sunlight and maintain the natural shape. Heading cuts (shearing and pinching are variations on heading) can cause lush growth but can ruin the natural shape of a tree or shrub. When you shear a formal hedge, it needs to be taken back just a few inches so it will not have bare spots. Always leave the bottom a little wider than the top to keep the growth lush down to the ground.

Roses

Roses can be a little confusing to prune but are generally very hardy and tolerant of imperfect pruning. At worst you may lose a few blooms. It helps to know what kind of rose you have:

- Climbers, once established, need only dead, weak or diseased wood removed in early spring. Other pruning should be right after they finish blooming.
- Old garden roses can be thinned a bit after bloom by cutting out unproductive branches.
- Floribundas, hybrid teas and grandifloras benefit by pruning in very early spring, just as the buds swell. Cut just above an outward facing bud twelve to twenty-four inches tall. You want to remove growth from the center and any crossing branches. When you are through, the plant should have three to six canes in a vase shape. As the season progresses, you should remove spent blooms down to an outward facing leaf with at least five leaflets to keep the plant blooming and open in the center. Always remove suckers that come from the rootstock.

Wisteria

Wisteria blooms on last year's spent bloom stock, called spurs. If you are randomly pruning to keep growth in check, you may have cut off the spurs. From late summer on, remove only the long tendrils that cascade out in all directions. If you need to keep the plant to a particular size, cut the ends but beware of shearing it. This year when it blooms, observe carefully where the flowers are and you will know what not to cut in subsequent years. If yours doesn't bloom, visit the Marin Art and Garden Center to observe a beautiful wisteria and study the bloom structure. Wisteria needs little fertilizer and can actually perform better if a little stressed—remember that plants bloom to reproduce and if conditions aren't great, they will attempt to set seed as a way to ensure survival of subsequent generations. Stay away from fertilizers with too much nitrogen (the first number of the three numbers on the bag or box) as it encourages green growth, not flowering.

Hydrangeas

Hydrangeas bloom on last season's growth, so they should be pruned after summer bloom. During the summer, as the blooms fade, you can cut those canes down low on the main branches and new growth will form that will bloom next year. A young plant can be left unpruned and will bloom well for a couple of years, but eventually will benefit from having canes removed to prevent it from becoming too leggy.

Oaks

Deciduous oaks should be pruned during the dormant season (December and January in the Bay area) and only to remove dead, damaged or diseased branches. Sometimes a light thinning of no more than ten to twenty percent of the leaf canopy can improve light penetration and reduce wind resistance. Too much pruning can cause sprouting all over the branches and this sprouting is very susceptible to mildew damage. Coast live oaks and other evergreen oaks are best pruned in July and August.

Tree-Trimming Technique

Sometimes it's useful to hire a registered arborist and watch how he prunes your tree and then keep it up from there. The vertical shoots are called water sprouts and should be removed. You may remove any growth along the lower trunk and any crossing or rubbing branches should be taken out.

Any large branches to be taken should be cut using the three-step technique that will prevent tearing the bark down the trunk:

1. About six to eight inches out from the trunk, make a cut from the bottom of the branch up about a third of the way into the branch.

2. Another six to ten inches out, cut off the entire branch.
3. Then cut the stub just outside the "collar" in line with the trunk. The idea is to leave the smallest area exposed, without a stub that invites disease. If properly cut, the wound will heal quite quickly. The University of California does not recommend painting the cuts with anything as this practice can encourage disease.

Planning Ahead

Pruning can be minimized by following this basic rule for the well-planned garden: plant with the mature size of the plant in mind. For example, photinia and myoporum, both fast growing, excellent plants for the Bay area, vary in size from about a foot to thirty-five feet tall, so careful selection of variety is essential to prevent a maintenance nightmare. Don't plant that nice gallon *Photinia serrulata* next to the sidewalk under a low window and commit yourself to monthly pruning if you want to see the view.

CHAPTER FIVE

Specialized Gardening

Tea Gardens

BY I'LEE HOOKER

Tea and gardens go together. You can have tea in the garden, or you can have a garden dedicated to herbs that make tea. "Taking tea" evokes images of a more leisurely era. An English tea conjures up thoughts of days gone by, with formal tables set in the garden in the late afternoon, under a spreading oak tree, with borders of abundant flowers nearby. A beautiful and highly polished silver tea service would adorn the table, complemented by delicious little cakes and finger sandwiches of watercress and cucumber. Who can forget the Mad Hatter's tea party in Alice in Wonderland and its wonderful commentary on the seriousness with which Victorian England took its tea?

In Japan, the relationship of tea and gardens historically developed as an important spiritual element of Zen Buddhism. The gardens offer a place where the Japanese can meditate and reflect on the spiritual connection of man to nature. Often there is a teahouse situated within the garden where the tea ceremony is performed. The view of the garden from the teahouse is intentionally arranged to encourage and enhance meditation. Each object used in the tea ceremony from the tea bowl and teapot to the tea itself is infused with special history and meaning. A woman will study for many years to be rewarded the honor of performing a tea ceremony. It is a special treat to experience a real tea ceremony and very difficult to find the opportunity. A wonderful place to have a simple cup of tea is the Japanese Tea Garden in Golden Gate Park. It is magical in the spring when the cherry blossoms and azaleas are in bloom.

~ Specialized Gardening ~

CREATING A TEA GARDEN

A tea garden is as much a state of mind as an actual location. It's a retreat that encourages you to relax and let go of the anxieties of the day and the stresses produced by our busy lives. It's where you can have a quiet conversation with a friend or two in an intimate setting.

Look for an area of your garden where you can create a space that feels private. It is comforting to have a tree, plantings or structure in back of you to provide a sense of enclosure. If it isn't a self-contained area, try to incorporate a view of the rest of the garden, or if you live in a hilly area, a view of water or mountains. Add a small table, a few chairs and a pot of tea and you have a simple tea garden.

HERBS FOR TEA

There is a wide range of herbs to choose from and our local nurseries are now stocking a fabulous collection appropriate for teas. Mint (*Mentha*) is always welcome because it blends well with other herbs or your favorite black or green tea. Remember mint is an invasive plant so always grow it in a container. It comes in almost as many flavors as Baskin-Robbins: peppermint, spearmint, pineapple mint, ginger mint, chocolate mint, lemon mint, orange bergamot mint, apple mint, licorice mint which is also called anise hyssop (*Agastache foeniculum*).

Fresh citrus adds a lively flavor and aroma to any tea: lemon balm (*Melissa officinalis*), lemon verbena (*Aloysia triphylla*), lemon grass (*Cymbopogon citralus*), Mrs. Burns lemon basil (*O. basilicum citriodora*) and lemon thyme. From your garden you can add fruity flavors from the rose family: rose hips or blackberry, strawberry or raspberry leaves. Of course, no herbal tea aficionado would be without chamomile. The type used the most for tea is an annual, German chamomile (*Matricaria recutita*). Three herbs that act as natural sweeteners are stevia (*Stevia rebaudiana*), Aztec sweet (*Lippia dulcis*) and sweet cicely (*Myrrhis odoratat*). A few savory herbs you may already have in your garden or can beg from a neighbor are rosemary, lavender, and pineapple sage (*Salvia elegans*). To add a little color and subtle flavor, use some of the golden petals of pot marigold (*Calendula officinalis*). Other easy additives are dried or fresh lemon and orange zest and fresh grated or dried gingerroot. If you have a smattering of these plants either on your deck in pots or in your garden, you already have a great selection of herbs to blend into your own fragrant and delicious teas.

Dried Versus Fresh Herbs

Dried herbs from your garden are very convenient to have on hand in the kitchen, but there is quite a lot of preparation involved in drying and storing your own herbs. It's very easy and satisfying to go out and snip your herbs, throw them in a teapot and add boiling water. You will eventually figure out the strength of tea that best suits you by trial and error, but you might start with one teaspoon of dried herbs or one tablespoon of fresh herbs to one cup of boiling water. Let the mixture steep from two to five minutes. It's great fun to make these teas in a glass teapot. Not only can you watch the infusion; you can also gauge the strength of the brew.

Recipes

- To equal amounts of ginger mint and lemon balm, add a couple sprigs of lemon basil.
- To taste, combine rosemary, lavender and lemon verbena. (wonderfully aromatic!)
- To chamomile add lemon balm and a few lavender buds.
- Steep with gunpowder tea (green tea that comes in little balls) any of the mints, especially orange bergamot mint, and fresh or dried rose petals. Caution: gunpowder tea gets very strong after steeping more than three minutes.

Container Gardening

by Kathy Reiffenstein

Just because you live in a condo with a long, narrow, bowling alley deck or an apartment with a postage stamp patio, that's no excuse not to garden! In fact, these outdoor spaces, somewhat removed from "terra firma," provide a wonderful opportunity to enjoy nature. Containers in all shapes and sizes allow you to cultivate flowers, herbs, even fresh veggies in the smallest of spaces.

Before getting down to digging and planting, take some time to think about what sort of a look and feel you want to achieve in your garden. Do you simply want some color that you can enjoy from inside? Do you want a quiet oasis, where you can sit and read among sweet scents and lush greenery? Do you want the look of an English garden, filled with all shapes and sizes of flowers, overflowing their containers, with barely enough room to squeeze by? Do you want the minimalism and simple elegance of a Japanese garden? Or do you want a formal look, with neat plants and classic containers, all highly organized in symmetrical arrangements? Answering these questions first will make for a much more productive trip to the nursery.

Another bit of homework that you need to do before you get started is to observe the weather and the microclimates on your deck or balcony. How much sun do you get a day? Is it morning or afternoon sun? Are there shady spots? For how long? How much wind do you get? Is it generally warm or cool? It is critical that you know the weather conditions in your garden to end up with the right plants. Although one huge benefit of a container garden is that you can move the pots to take advantage of shifting sun or shade, you want to maximize your success by choosing the best possible plants for your specific location.

Containers

There is virtually nothing that can't be used as a planter, as long as it has drainage holes and can survive outside. If you do fall in love with a container that doesn't have drainage holes, you can drill your own (use an electric drill with a masonry bit for clay and concrete) or use it as an outer, decorative pot, and put a smaller draining planter inside. Just make sure you don't let the inner pot sit in water: empty excess water.

Planters run the gamut from traditional terra cotta to wood to ceramic to plastic to concrete to whimsical items such as an old pail, a watering can or an old rubber boot. Your imagination's the limit!

Keep your style in mind as you consider various containers. An old rubber boot probably won't really fit in your formal garden, unless you are looking to add an amusing note. Most nurseries and home improvement stores stock standard plastic terra cotta look-alike, genuine terra cotta and ceramic. To find other, more unusual containers, search out garage sales, antique shops or your parents' attic. Also think about how well the container will complement the plant you're putting in it. A good rule to follow is that if the container is quite elaborate or bold in design, keep the planting simple; if the pot is simple and basic, you can go for a more dramatic plant.

Aside from the look, different materials hold water differently. Keep this in mind as you think about how much attention you'll pay to your garden. Terra cotta and untreated wood are the most porous; they will allow air to get to the roots, and water and fertilizer to move out through the container walls. But they will require frequent watering since they will dry out quickly. Glazed ceramic and plastic containers tend to retain moisture, so you will need to be careful that you don't over water or over fertilize.

No matter what kind of container you choose, before planting, clean it out thoroughly with household bleach and water (one part bleach to ten parts water). Also, be sure to raise your container up off the ground, once it's planted. It only needs to be an inch or so off the ground to promote good drainage and air circulation, as well as prevent water stains on decks and balconies. You can put bricks or blocks of wood beneath your pots (be sure to position them so that air can reach the drainage hole) or you can purchase decorative feet at nurseries. Another inexpensive solution is to purchase the tiny, three-inch pot saucers at the nursery and turn them upside down under your plant. Three small saucers provide a stable perch for most pots.

Choosing Plants

Almost any plant will be happy in a container, as long as the container is big enough and the growing conditions are appropriate. However, a container does restrict a plant and makes it almost wholly dependent on you for its water and nutrients. Plants well suited to living in a container have:

- a naturally compact growth habit
- attractive foliage
- flowers for a long time (or repeat flowers)
- low water requirements

Annuals, perennials, grasses, bulbs, shrubs, vines, herbs and veggies will all do well in containers. If you're buying perennials, don't fill the pot, because they'll grow and before you know it, you'll have to repot. Instead, add some colorful annuals to fill in around perennials until they fill out.

Consider using color and texture in a container for added impact. Mass a number of the same plants or combine several different plants of the same color family for drama; for example, fill up a container with trailing purple-blue convolvulus (*Convolvulus sabatius*) or pair up orangey-yellow black-eyed Susans (*Rudbeckia fulgida* 'Goldstrum') and lemon yellow coreopsis (*Coreopsis verticillata* 'Moonbeam'). Match up a cool pastel plant with gray-green grasses or foliage: lavender or pink scabiosa (*Scabiosa caucasica*) with licorice plant (*Helichrysum petiolare*) and lambs ears (*Stachys byzantina*). Or mix plants with opposite colors on the color wheel: purple New England asters (*Aster novi-angliae* 'Purple Dome') and yellow marigolds (*Tagetes*).

Soil

The right growing medium will be critical to the success of your plants. It is best to use a good organic potting soil from your nursery, as regular garden soil is way too dense to use in containers. Potting soil is lighter, fast draining and contains numerous nutrients and mineral matter; if you choose potting soil specially formulated for containers, you won't need to add any other ingredients. Place a piece of shade cloth or plastic mesh over the drainage hole(s) so the soil won't run out each time you water. Be sure to thoroughly water the soil once you've put it into the container and before you plant.

Care

Now that you have chosen your plants, matched them up with containers that will show off their beauty, and artfully arranged them, it's time to focus on taking care of them. Care of a container garden is not all that different from an in-ground garden, except that plants in containers are almost completely reliant on you for their moisture and nutrients.

Watering

Watering your pots faithfully is the most important aspect of container gardening. Because your plants are confined to pots, they can't draw moisture from the surrounding soil like in-ground plants and tend to need more frequent watering. Check the moisture level of your plants often—the easiest way is to stick your finger in the pot. If the top inch of soil feels dry, you should water. Lightweight potting soil, terra cotta containers and warm or windy weather all tend to make your plants dry out more quickly. Check the moisture requirements for each of your plants, as some plants prefer constantly moist soil, while others can go dry between waterings. Be sure to mulch, using bark, straw, cocoa bean hulls or almond shells. This will prevent the soil from drying out and, if the mulch is organic, will add nutrients to the soil as it breaks down.

~ *Specialized Gardening* ~

When you water your containers, give them a good drenching. When water runs freely from the drainage holes, you'll know you've saturated the soil. If you have saucers under your plants, be sure to empty them once the water has drained through or the soil will stay too soggy.

If your container garden is not too large, it is a good idea to water everything by hand. That way, you can ensure that each plant gets exactly the amount of water it needs, and you can check for insects and diseases at the same time. A large number of pots or a too busy gardener necessitate a drip irrigation system to ensure that your containers are adequately and consistently watered.

Fertilizing

The only nutrients your container plants are going to get are the ones you give them, so it is a good idea to fertilize when the plants are actively growing from spring though fall. That said, be wary of over fertilizing, particularly with high nitrogen fertilizers which cause rapid growth and, in turn, tend to attract pests such as aphids.

Read and follow fertilizer package directions, although it may be wise to give your plants a half-strength dose and see how they do, thus minimizing the chances of over fertilizing. A slow release fertilizer, in contrast to a liquid fertilizer, will allow the plant to take up what it needs over a period of time, rather than giving it a concentrated "hit" all at once. Fertilizers are an area where you really need to talk with your nursery professional and experiment in your own garden to see what works best for you.

Pest Management

Pests and diseases will be less frequent visitors to your container garden if you keep your plants healthy and happy—give them the right growing conditions and water and feed them adequately. Deadhead your plants frequently and clean up any fallen debris in the pots; don't over fertilize; check regularly for initial signs of any problem.

If you do find some insects on your plants, treat immediately and use the least toxic method of control possible: hose off aphids with a strong stream of water; hand-pick slugs and snails and dispose of them; hang yellow sticky strips to catch whiteflies; plant yarrow, dill, cosmos, and alyssum to attract beneficial insects (like lady beetles) which eat the harmful insects.

Pruning

To ensure that your plants produce as many flowers as possible, cut or pinch off (deadhead) spent blooms regularly. Some plants, such as roses, need to be pruned each year, generally in January. Let the look of your plant be the guide as to whether or not you need to prune—if the plant appears straggly or is producing stunted-looking flowers or fruit, prune it back by about one-third to encourage new growth. Most plants can be pruned in the fall, after the growing season.

Finishing Touches

To put the finishing touches on your garden, add a few decorative elements intermingled with the plants. Consider small, whimsical concrete statues, such as frogs or turtles, metal plant sticks in various designs, a stone Buddha or painted garden signs, proclaiming "A Garden is the Happiest Place on Earth".

Herbs in Your Own Backyard

by I'Lee Hooker

If you were to look at your garden through the eyes of an herbalist, your garden might very well look to him like a well-stocked medicine chest. What kind of herbs would he find and how would he use them?

In Bay area gardens, we grow a number of herbs and weave them into our landscape for a variety of reasons. Many of the aromatic herbs, like sage, rosemary, thyme and oregano are deer resistant. This is important, because in the Bay area an unfenced garden is an open invitation for our hungry deer to dine. Many plants that are staples of our dry, Mediterranean climate are actually herbs, such as rosemary, lavender, artemesia and yarrow. Long before they became fashionable in herbal remedies, hypericum was used as a ground cover and echinacea was a favorite late summer perennial for the border. There are even common flowers worth exploring for their medicinal value. Remember, though, it is inadvisable to use any herbs for medicinal reasons without consulting your doctor or a certified herbalist.

Common Garden Herbs

Yarrow (*Achillea millefolium*)

Yarrow is native to Europe and in classic times was known as herba militaris because it was used during battles to staunch the flow of blood from wounds. The plant is named after Achilles because he is reputed to have used it to heal the wounds of his soldiers.

Wormwood (*Artemisia absinthium*)

This bitter tasting herb (*absinthium* means "without sweetness") addresses digestive problems. Its strong aromatic properties made it one of the main flavorings for vermouth and other alcoholic drinks.

St. John's Wort (*Hypericum perforatum*)
Medieval Europeans believed this herb had magical qualities. The flowers were harvested at the summer solstice and were used to ward off evil. Most people today are aware of its value as an antidepressant.

Lavender (*Lavandula officinalis* and *L. angustifolia*)
Lavender is highly regarded for its sweet-scented aroma. Matanzas Creek Winery in the Sonoma Valley has made a profitable secondary business from harvesting its lavender and making soaps, perfumes, and essential oils. In the Middle Ages, lavender was highly prized for its ability to relieve headaches and calm nervous tension. The early pilgrims brought it to this country in 1620. Contemporary research has shown lavender oil to be an effective antiseptic, promoting healing of burns, wounds, sores, and relieving insect bites.

Rosemary (*Rosmarinus officinalis*)
Rosemary is native to southern Europe and a favorite ingredient in Mediterranean cooking. It has been well known since antiquity for its ability to improve memory. Greek students still burn it in their homes the night before they take exams. It is considered a warming herb because it stimulates circulation of blood to the brain, easing headache pain, especially migraine, and controlling fainting spells.

Feverfew (*Tanacetum parthenium*)
In 17th century England, it was considered the woman's herb, used to clean a woman's womb after birth and to strengthen her reproductive organs. Its name reflects its use in lowering body temperature and relieving fevers. Today it is considered an important herbal treatment for migraine headaches.

Echinacea or Purple coneflower (*Echinacea agustifolia* and *E. purpure*)
A North American native, echinacea has proven very effective in raising the body's resistance to bacterial and viral infections. The

~ *Specialized Gardening* ~

Comanche and Sioux used echinacea to cure sore throats, rabies, and snakebites. The herbal remedies are prepared from echinacea roots.

Calendula or Pot Marigold (*Calendula officinalis*)
Calendula is a versatile herb that is highly valued in Western herbal medicine today. It is an effective antiseptic used to treat many minor skin irritations such as minor burns, diaper rash, fungal conditions and acne. The bright orange petals are harvested in summer and made into infused oils, tinctures and infusions.

Passionflower (*Passiflora incarnata*)
Another native of North America, passionflower was used by the Algonquin people as a tranquilizer. It is a valuable sedative and is prescribed in herbal medicine for insomnia, epilepsy, and hysteria.

Nasturtium (*Tropaeolum majus*)
Nasturtiums are native to Peru. They are grown as ornamental plants and the leaves and flowers are used in salads. The indigenous peoples of the Andes used nasturtium as a medicinal disinfectant and to heal wounds. It is very high in vitamin C and all aerial parts of the plant are edible and have a slightly pungent flavor.

Heartsease (*Viola tricolor*)
This little viola has an herbal history that goes back many centuries. In 1735, Keogh mentioned in his *Irish Herbal* that heartsease flowers "cure convulsions in children, cleanse the lungs and breast and are very good for fevers, internal inflammations and wounds." It is not valued today for its medicinal uses, but certainly makes an attractive addition to your salad.

Aloe (*Aloe vera*)
Keep a pot of aloe near your house. The clear gel that emerges when you crack a leaf contains aloectin B. It puts a protective coating over wounds, ulcers, and burns and greatly speeds up healing time.

CHAPTER SIX

Habitat Gardening

Habitat Gardening

by Maggie Agro

It's been an especially hectic week and, driving home, you wish for a refuge where you can sit quietly and listen to a pond gurgling or birds singing. A quiet place where you can watch the butterflies and hear the calming sounds of nature, a private nest to envelop you.

What you need is your own personal habitat. "A place where people, plants and wildlife live harmoniously and naturally," as authors Nancy Bauer and Lyn Howe describe it in *Habitat Gardening— Putting the Pieces Back Together*. You can create such a place in your own garden.

If this idea seems like it might be a big project or it may take too much work, think again. You probably already have the beginnings of a habitat garden. First of all, observe what birds and insects your plantings currently attract. Then take another small step.

Try a little benign neglect by allowing a small part of your garden to "go wild". Put off cutting summer plants back. Late flowering plants, if left alone, will go to seed and provide food for seed-eating birds such as the finch, titmouse and grosbeak. Don't remove all of your leaf litter. Leave a little brush pile that can serve as a shelter for beneficial insects or insectivores, such as ladybugs, ground beetles and soldier beetles, or provide cover and nesting materials for birds.

Do you have a clean water source for birds? It can be as simple as a plant saucer filled daily with fresh water and placed off the ground, near trees or shrubs to provide cover from neighborhood cats. If cats are a problem, attach a bell to your cat's collar and ask your neighbors to do the same with their cats.

If you wish to take it a step further, in the fall you can add one or two plants specifically for birds. The blooms of flowering perennials and annuals attract insects for insectivores and provide food for nectar eaters.

If you love roses, try planting wild roses, *Rosa californica*, with their fragrant deep pink flowers. Not only do the rose hips provide nutrients for birds, but the shrub thickets also provide sites for ground nesters and quail. Native roses are more resistant to disease and fungus, as well as being more fragrant than cultivars.

California fuchsia, (*Epilobium*, formerly *Zauschneria californica*), a native perennial groundcover that grows in partial to full sun and dry soil, produces scarlet trumpet-shaped flowers that bloom in fall and attract hummingbirds.

Evening primrose, (*Oenothera hookeri*), a native biennial, perfect for the back of a sunny dry border, provides stunning, sunny yellow saucer-shaped flowers, whose seed pods open slowly, offering one seed a day. It attracts goldfinches, juncos and California finches. Bees and other pollinators drink its nectar.

Try sunflowers that love full sun, work in any soil, need little water and have a long bloom period. They provide pollen for butterflies and seed for juncos and sparrows.

The list of native plants that would be ideal habitat plants is extensive. Most provide beauty for your garden, are easy to maintain and attract birds, butterflies and "good bugs" precisely because they grow naturally in our area. They are adapted to our climate and do not need special care or fertilizers. The ideal time to plant natives is in the fall after the rains begin.

If you don't have room for trees and shrubs, add vines like trumpet, honeysuckle and wild grape for birds and pollinators.

Fennel, parsley, carrots, Queen Anne's lace and dill (all members of the Family called Umbelliferae) will attract the "good bugs" that will eat the aphids and other "bad bugs" in your garden. If you let them go to seed, umbellifers will also attract birds.

Try a small compost pile to attract worms as well as provide nutrients for your soil.

By taking these small steps, in your own private way you are creating something unique—an ecosystem of which you are both benefactor and grateful recipient. You are building your own personal habitat.

Butterfly Gardens

by Nancy Bauer

Mariposa, papillon, borboleta, babochka, the butterfly is a symbol of beauty in any language. These little miracles of transformation, however, like so many of nature's offerings, are showing signs of.distress. Loss of habitat is the main culprit. With butterfly counts decreasing, it couldn't be a better time to offer your garden as sanctuary and, in turn, reward yourself with fascinating visitors in many disguises.

The name of the game in butterfly gardening, of course, is planting for the caterpillar, too. Here is a wonderful opportunity to see the intimate and crucial relationship between plants and insects. While the adult butterfly will feed from many different nectar sources, the butterfly caterpillar is nourished by only a few plants, and in some cases, just one. The Monarch lays her eggs only on milkweed; the Pipevine Swallowtail's only caterpillar food plant is Dutchman's pipe. Some host plants, thistles, wild radish, fennel, clover, nettles, and cheeseweed grow wild in meadows, in yards, and by the side of the road. Knowing how important they are to some of our local butterflies, you may feel a little friendlier toward them and allow places for them to grow undisturbed. Many native trees, shrubs, wildflowers and vines are caterpillar food plants or nectar sources and most can be grown in backyard gardens.

To beckon the butterflies, follow these simple habitat basics:

- mass colorful, fragrant nectar-rich flowers in a sunny area
- place caterpillar food plants near the nectar plants
- be careful when pruning and raking—chrysalides and butterfly eggs hide in shrubs, and brush piles, on twigs and leaves
- provide a shallow saucer or muddy spot for moisture
- avoid pesticides

Planting for a few of the most common local butterflies is a good way to start. The Painted Lady and West Coast Lady use many species of the mallow family as host plants, but the best choices are native *lavatera* or checkerbloom (*Sidalcea malvaeflora*). Bronze fennel, lovage (an herb) or parsley massed near the vegetable garden or other sunny spot will attract the black and yellow Anise Swallowtail, which likes members of the umbellifer family. Plant snapdragons, linaria, and monkey flowers for the orange and brown Buckeye; milkweed in the summer for Monarchs (*Asclepias* spp.).

California buckeye are host plants for a dozen local butterflies. Ceanothus feeds six butterfly caterpillars. Skippers, tiny butterflies in earth-tone colors, use bunch grasses and carex for host plants. Especially if you live near a wooded stream or forest, consider planting willows (Lorquin's Admiral, Western Tiger Swallowtail), nettles (Red Admiral) and Dutchman's pipe (Pipevine Swallowtail).

Butterflies love the nectar-rich flowers of the daisy family: asters, coreopsis, purple coneflower, cosmos, zinnia, yarrow. They are also attracted to tightly clustered tubular flowers such as statice, lantana, rosemary, the salvias and verbenas.

Don't forget medicinal and culinary herbs. They are some of the best nectar plants for all beneficial insects, including butterflies.

Aim to have nectar plants blooming in all seasons. For fall bloom, try goldenrod, sedum Autumn Joy, or Michaelmas daisy. It's better to mass several good nectar plants than plant just a few each of many different varieties. If you are mixing natives and non-natives, be sure they are culturally compatible. Most butterfly habitat plants are, by nature, hardy, sun-loving and low water use plants. Growing a butterfly habitat couldn't be easier: no fussy plants to worry over, no garden design rules to follow. If you already have good nectar plants, add host plants for common butterflies. Continue to mass nectar plants in your sunniest areas. In the fall, plant native trees or shrubs, perennials or wildflowers. Most important, have fun. This could easily be the most rewarding gardening experience you will ever have.

Where Have All the Songbirds Gone?

by Diane Lynch

Does your garden seem to lack the presence of chattering birds? Over the last few decades scientists have documented that the number of songbirds is declining. When one considers the biological feat that migration represents, it is understandable that seemingly small decreases in habitat can make a big difference in bird numbers. Birds weighing mere ounces must feed voraciously to put on body fat to enable them to make the journey from as far north as breeding grounds in Canada to South America, where many winter. Some of these tiny creatures travel nonstop for up to eighty-five hours, making a triathlon seem trifling in comparison. When they arrive at their destinations they are exhausted, emaciated and in need of instant nourishment and rest. This is true at each end of the migratory path. Other birds take a more leisurely trip north or south, stopping along the way to feed and rest.

Many aspects of migration aren't well understood, but we do know that loss of habitat is critical. We all know about the rainforests being leveled to graze cattle for our hamburgers and grow coffee to satisfy our coffee cravings. We can ask our grocers and coffee shops to stock shade grown coffee, which is grown without leveling forests, and we could eat a veggieburger now and then. We continue to lose habitat in the United States as we build more and more subdivisions. Of course, people need places to live as our population increases, but we need to give serious thought to better urban planning to preserve critical forests and other habitat such as grasslands. When forests are fragmented by development, opportunistic species such as the brown-headed cowbird thrive. Cowbirds lay their eggs in the nests of smaller birds and when the eggs hatch, the larger cowbirds are reared by the unsuspecting hosts and out-compete the rightful babies. We in the Bay area are lucky to live in a place that has some of the best urban planning in the world. For example, the western part of Marin County has been preserved as parkland or for agricultural use, preserving critical habitats.

The Bay area is on the Pacific flyway and is an important wintering and breeding ground for many species of migratory waterfowl, songbirds, raptors and shorebirds. We have many birds that breed in the Bay area as well as many species that winter in California and then breed elsewhere. In early spring, the migrating waterfowl start to leave the Bay to head north to breed. Among the songbirds that fly north to breed in the Bay area are the white-throated swift, black-chinned hummingbird, Allen's hummingbird, olive-sided flycatcher, western wood-pewee, Pacific-slope flycatcher, purple martin, violet-green swallow, barn swallow, house wren, blue-gray gnatcatcher, Swainson's thrush, solitary vireo, warbling vireo, orange-crowned warbler, yellow warbler, hermit warbler, Wilson's warbler, western tanager, lark sparrow, grasshopper sparrow, hooded oriole and northern oriole.

One thing these birds have in common is that many survive largely on insects, which makes them welcome in most gardens as they scarf up caterpillars and flying insects. Some, such as hummingbirds, are pollinators. Some birds certainly feed on the seed in feeders but a lot of gardeners complain that the seed germinates and creates weed problems. Niger thistle seed doesn't germinate and it attracts small birds such as finches. More important than putting seed out is to consider planting natives that either feed birds directly or provide shelter and nesting sites. Native plants do the best job of providing food and shelter for our native birds. Plant a coffeeberry, toyon, flowering currant, ceanothus, elderberry or other wonderful California native to feed or shelter the birds. Many bird species are dependent on the habitat provided by native vegetation and taken all together, home plantings can enhance the bird populations in our area.

~ *Habitat Gardening* ~

Limit the poisons you use in the garden. Everything you spray has a wider effect than you might imagine since a large percentage of the bugs in the garden are actually beneficial and many sprays are nondiscriminatory. Many birds are very sensitive to the toxic effects of insecticides and most of the Bay area drains to the Bay, sending these pollutants into the waters inhabited by shorebirds and waterfowl. Indiscriminate use of pesticides usually does more harm than good in the long run.

The most obvious predator in suburban areas is the common house cat. At least equip your cat with a bell and consider keeping him indoors during the spring breeding season. Spay or neuter your cat and call the humane society if you have feral cats living nearby.

Millions of birds are needlessly killed each year when they crash into windows. Do the birds a favor and save your furniture from fading at the same time by closing blinds or curtains in unused rooms or when you are gone.

Berries for the Birds

~

BY DIANE LYNCH

Your garden, no matter how small, can be a place of beauty and respite for you as well as a smorgasbord for the birds. There are dozens of trees and shrubs that will provide shelter and food for them. Usually natives are best since they evolved to feed the native birds, but there are exotics which thrive in the Bay area and aren't too invasive.

Think in terms of what birds need when you are changing your garden or adding plants: food, water, shelter and a place to raise young. Understory plants grow between trees and lawn and both feed and create habitat for birds.

Doreen Smith of the California Native Plant Society put together a great list of plants for birds. These are some of the small trees and large shrubs she recommends which provide berries and seeds and, when flowering, nectar for hummingbirds:

- Holly-leaf cherry (*Prunus ilicifolia*) and the Catalina cherry (*Prunus lyonii*)—both favored by robins, finches, towhees and cedar waxwings.
- Coffeeberry (*Rhamnus californica*) comes in varieties that range from one to fifteen feet in height and produces black juicy fruit for thrushes, jays, mockingbirds, robins, band-tailed pigeons and purple finches.
- Toyon (*Heteromeles arbutifolia*) fruits on year old wood, providing red berries for waxwings, quail, towhees, Western bluebird, robins, mockingbirds, band-tailed pigeons. There are beautiful coffeeberries and toyons around the parking lot at Blackie's Pasture in Tiburon.
- California wax myrtle (*Myrica californica*) is one of our best looking natives with glossy, fragrant foliage that looks great

~ *Habitat Gardening* ~

all year. It can grow to thirty feet, but can be kept as a hedge, and has waxy nutlets favored by flickers, finches and robins.
- Ceanothus comes in many sizes and provides great cover as well as seeds for bushtits, mockingbrids, quail and finches.
- Elderberries (*Sambucus* spp.) are very tasty to many birds as well as being host to beneficial insects. They can be pruned to an understory tree or left as a rangy bush.
- Willows (*Salix* spp.) and native roses (*Rosa californica*) are great host and bird plants but are best planted in an area to be left wild.
- Manzanita (*Arctostaphylos* spp.) produce charming bell shaped blooms in winter, which mature to little apple (thus the name) shaped fruits which attract robins, waxwings and mockingbirds as well as providing shelter for quail.
- Oregon grape (*Mahonia aquifolium* and other spp.) is a beautiful shrub with bright yellow flowers followed by blue fruit, enjoyed by finches, towhees, robins.
- Red and pink flowering currants or gooseberries (*Ribes sanguineum*) start to bloom in February. They produce berries for many birds and their flowers are especially savored by hummingbirds.

In general, the more species you can plant in your garden, the more likely you are to attract birds. Try to mimic nature and plant diverse areas as you create your own ecosystem. Leave some piles of brush here and there for cover. In our mild climate we can dispense with birdfeeders if we have food available in the garden in the form of flowers for hummingbirds and fruits for other birds.

Winter is a good planting time. Its increased rainfall gives plants a good start before our long dry summer. Do the birds a favor and go to your favorite nursery and buy a few plants to fill in blank spots in the garden—they will thank you with their cheery presence in the years to come.

CHAPTER SEVEN

Flowering Plants

Scented Geraniums, Actually Pelargoniums

by Diane Lynch

Looking for a plant that the deer don't like, smells great, has interesting foliage and flowers all year and doesn't require much care? Look no further than the scented geranium, which is actually a pelargonium. So what's the difference? Scented geranium is the common name for members of the family Geraniaceae, genus *Pelargonium*, which includes many species, some scented and others not. Pelargonium comes from the Greek *pelargos* for "stork" and geranium is a modification of the Greek *geranion* meaning "cranes bill". These names suggest the elongated, beaklike seed cases they bear. Although mistakenly called geraniums, pelargoniums are easily recognized by their flower structure. Like geraniums, each blossom will have five petals, but in pelargoniums the petals are arranged with two upper petals and three lower. The upper two are often larger and more richly colored. In true geraniums the five petals are evenly formed and spaced.

There are anywhere from fifty to two hundred and fifty cultivars depending on whom you choose to believe; the consensus seems to be that there are about seventy-five left from the two hundred and fifty for which there are records. Unusual foliage varies from fine fernlike leaves to round saucer-shaped leaves. Colors range from green and gray-green to variegations with white and other colors. Most have small insignificant blooms but some such as 'Clorinda' and 'Mrs. Kingsley' have spectacular flowers. All are evergreen.

The scented pelargonium is prized for its incredible range of scents, released by the sun as well as by brushing the plant. Scents run the gamut from rose, mint, lemon, fruit, nut, spice, to pungent. Some, like chocolate pelargonium, require a little imagination to experience. The French recognized the economic potential of scented pelargoniums in the nineteenth century when they discovered that the aromatic oils could be substituted for the expensive attar of roses used to make perfume; the oil is actually twice as strong but nearly identical to the real attar of *Rosa damascena*. Beginning in 1819, fields of rose scented pelargoniums sprang up in southern France and later in Kenya, Corsica, Algeria, Turkey, Spain and Italy. Oils extracted from scented pelargoniums have been used in Italy and France to scent soaps, tooth powders and ointments. A pound of leaves will produce a gram of oil. Leaves can be crushed and used to scent rooms, as well as dried for use in potpourri.

In their native South Africa, scented pelargoniums can grow into treelike shrubs with heights of ten feet or more. Parts of South Africa have a Mediterranean climate much like the Bay area, so their water needs are minimal. The essential oils produced in glands at the base of tiny leaf hairs shield them from the intense sun in their native South Africa as well as protect them from predators. They grow well in containers as well as in the garden. They are hardy to about 25°F, so in our climate they usually make it through the winter outside and can grow into a sizeable shrub. In fact, our coastal climate provides ideal conditions for scented pelargoniums: 50°F-60°F at night, 65°F-75°F during the day. They aren't as happy when temperatures regularly go above 90°F. They prefer light, well-drained soil in sun to part shade.

Pruning will encourage dense growth and is essential to keep container grown plants under control. They do not like soggy roots or water on foliage in cloudy conditions. They like regular but not excessive water and will lose bottom leaves if left too dry but they usually recover readily. Over fertilizing will yield fat plants with sparse, buxom leaves. They are susceptible to very few pests; whiteflies, aphids, spider mites and mealybugs occur infrequently and usually only on indoor plants. Diseases can usually be avoided by giving them reasonable care: good ventilation and regular water. Overall,

Flowering Plants

scented pelargoniums are tolerant of a somewhat negligent gardener who doesn't water or fertilize much.

Scented pelargoniums have several uses in the kitchen. Fresh leaves of rose pelargoniums can be added to tea. They can be cooked and the fragrant oils used in puddings and custards. Some can be used to flavor cakes, jellies, fruit punches, ice cream, vinegars and sorbets. Rose scented varieties are the most widely used for flavoring purposes but others can be used also.

To flavor a cake, place clean, unsprayed leaves in the bottom of a prepared cake pan just before pouring in the batter. Pull off the leaves and discard after the cake is baked and placed on a rack to cool. To flavor a jelly, put a leaf in each prepared jar just before pouring in hot jelly. Use light flavors such as apple to allow the flavor to be appreciated.

Interestingly, lemon-scented pelargoniums (*P. citriadora*) have been used to extract large amounts of heavy metals from soil. The plants tested by researchers at the University of Guelph, Ontario, exhibited no signs of toxicity or stress and appeared to be tolerant of a wide variety of toxic metals. These traits would make them potentially valuable in agriculture as well as in the remediation of polluted soils.

Scented pelargoniums are very easy to clone by rooting cuttings in damp potting soil. Rooting hormone will up your chances of success but is not really necessary. Share with friends and spread these great plants around the neighborhood.

The New Heucheras

~

BY I'LEE HOOKER

Do you remember the little perennial woodland plant *Heuchera sanquinea* of the family Saxifragaceae, commonly called coral bells? It was used as a filler plant with pleasant enough green basal leaves and either pink or red delicate bell shaped flowers on stems that rose a foot or so from the base. These plants made good ground cover under trees and were sometimes used as edging along the front of the border. Recently, there has been a dramatic change in the types of heuchera that are available. Dan Heims from Terra Nova Nursery in Oregon is the man most responsible for bringing these stunning foliage plants to our local nurseries through a rigorous breeding program. By combining the best of each heuchera species (*H. sanquinea, H. micrantha, H. richardsonii* and H. *americana*), he has produced plants that are varied in leaf structure and color, grow bigger and more colorful flowers, and are insect and mildew resistant. The name heuchera is of German origin and is pronounced "Hue-ker-a."

The new heucheras are a successful introduction into a plant market hungry for new varieties and colors. They are perfect at the front of the border where they can soften the edge of a pathway or gently cascade over a wall. For sheer drama they are hard to beat. By contrasting a dark maroon ruffled leaf heuchera like 'Plum Pudding' or 'Chocolate Ruffle' next to a lime colored leaf plant such as *Helichrysum petiolare* 'Limelight', feverfew 'Aureum', pelargonium 'Golden Staph' or ipomoea (sweet potato) 'Margarite' you can create an eye popping combination. The maroon heuchera as well as the silvery ones such as 'Pewter Moon' would make a superb combination with pink flowers such as pink dianthus or alstroemeria.

Heuchera 'Eco-Improved' is an exciting new introduction. In early spring, the new leaves are bronzy-green with maroon veins

~ *Flowering Plants* ~

followed by tiny white flowers on stalks that shoot up two feet. There are two good variegated white and green leaf heucheras: 'Splish-Splash' and 'Snow Angel'. New maroon varieties are being introduced all the time, with variations of tightly ruffled leaves, silver or maroon veining, bright burgundy or pink under leaf. The regular green leaf variety now comes in a spectrum of flower colors from white to fire red.

Heucheras do well in full sun areas where summers do not get really hot. Inland they would do best with at least half a day of shade. They are moderately drought tolerant and like loose well-drained soil, high in organic content, with a pH range from 6.5 to 7.7. The purple leaf varieties can take full sun in hotter areas if they have adequate water. If fabulous foliage is your goal, remove the flowers. It is often a choice between flowers and foliage because the plant will expend its energy on one or the other. In pots and containers they combine well with other plants and thrive in regular potting soil.

Heucheras are resistant to most pests and diseases. Snails like to hide in their leafy cover but don't find them very tasty. In the spring, you might find some orange rust on the under side of the leaves. Strip the plant of the diseased leaves and spray with a low-toxicity fungicide such as sulfur or Neem oil.

Spring is a good time to divide heucheras. It is also possible to propagate heuchera though leaf cuttings. Dip the stem in rooting hormone and root it in moist sand or vermiculite.

Hydrangea Hyperbole

by Kathy Reiffenstein

Hydrangeas are a popular plant in the Bay area and with good reason. They are lush, attractive, and, once established, easy to care for.

The *Hydrangea macrophylla*, big-leaf, garden or French hydrangea, part of the family Hydrangeaceae, is a deciduous shrub native to Asia. The word hydrangea comes from the Greek *hydor* meaning water and *aggeion* meaning vessel, so named because the seed capsules resemble a small water pitcher. *H. macrophylla* is also known as *H. hortensia, H. opuloides* and *H. otaksa*. Its many names are the result of the difficulties 18th century botanists had in attributing specimens to a particular family. The early specimens imported to Europe from China and Japan produced little sterile flowers that did not have any stamens that could be counted or seed capsules that could be studied.

Other species include the climbing hydrangea (*H. anomala*), the smooth hydrangea (*H. arborescens*), the roots of which are used in botanical medicine, the peegee hydrangea (*H. paniculata* 'Grandiflora') and the oak leaf hydrangea (*H. quercifolia*).

The big-leaf hydrangea is the familiar, "mop-headed" blue, pink or white species that is frequently seen. Its enormous blossom clusters look like pom-poms and may be eight to ten inches across, each cluster composed of a mass of one to one and one-half inch flowers that are sterile, that is, unable to produce seeds. A special category of big-leaf hydrangea is called lacecap because the flat four to eight-inch flower clusters are composed of fertile central blossoms surrounded by a "lace" of large, flat sterile blossoms. The big-leaf hydrangea has a symmetrical, rounded growth pattern and most garden plants become three to six feet tall. The plants have shiny, broadly ovate, coarsely toothed leaves that can be eight inches long, and bloom from June through October.

The big-leaf hydrangea remains attractive even after blooming, because the flower clusters—being composed of sepals and not petals—do not fall but remain on the plant until early winter. They often change to lovely shades of red, pink and green, and can easily be cut and dried for indoor use.

Hydrangeas are easy to grow in the right conditions. *H. macrophylla* performs well in areas where winters are fairly mild. It does well in seaside gardens and flourishes near the shore, so it is well-suited to the Mediterranean climate of the Bay area.

The big-leaf hydrangea will grow in full sun on the coast, but it is particularly suitable for shade. It prefers rich, porous soil that is constantly moist but well-drained, and therefore, would not be a good candidate for a drought-tolerant landscape.

The big-leaf hydrangea requires no regular pruning, except to remove dead flower heads and any dead wood. In the fall, after blooming, prune stems that bore flowers to just above the nearest outward facing bud. Any weak or badly formed growths and branches that seem too crowded together in the center of the plant can be removed, thus allowing light and air to penetrate. It is a mistake to cut big-leaf hydrangeas down to ground level or even to prune them severely.

H. macrophylla are generally trouble-free. Aphids, slugs and snails may occasionally feed on stems and foliage. Very alkaline soil conditions may cause chlorosis, with yellowing between the veins of the leaves, or very pale leaves and flowers.

Except for the white varieties, the color of the flowers is affected by the amount of aluminum in the soil available to the plant. Aluminum is present in all soils, but its availability to the plant depends on the acidity of the soil. Big-leaf hydrangeas require acid soil—pH 6.0 to 6.5 for pink flowers and a pH of 5.0 to 5.5 for blue ones. Some big-leaf hydrangeas switch from pink to blue flowers or vice-versa with a change of only one half point on their soil's pH scale.

Plants can be made or kept blue by applying aluminum sulfate to the soil. Treat the soil several times in the spring and fall at weekly intervals with one-quarter ounce of aluminum sulfate to a gallon of water. To obtain or keep pink flowers, add lime to the soil. You can also use fertilizers with a high percentage of phosphorus, which reacts with the aluminum contained in the soil, and the two elements combine in an insoluble form; thus, the aluminum is neutralized and the flowers remain, or become, pink. These treatments will likely not be effective unless they are started before the plant blooms.

Big-leaf hydrangeas make wonderful dried flower displays. Drying them slowly is the key. Once the flower clusters have turned the muted shades of fall, cut them and clip off any leaves or browned flowers. Smash the stems with a hammer to help them absorb water, and place them in a container with two inches of water. Leave the container in a cool spot out of the sun. The water will evaporate in a week or so and you will have an attractive bouquet of hydrangeas to enjoy throughout the winter.

Achilleas: Legends and Lore

by Barbara J. Euser

My first acquaintance with Achilleas was made in the Rocky Mountains. Growing alongside every trail was a wildflower with flattish white clusters of flowers and feathery gray-green leaves. It was yarrow, officially *Achillea millefolium*. I became fascinated by its many uses and the legends and lore surrounding it. Over the years, it has become a staple in my garden in Marin.

Yarrow is called *Achillea* because, according to legend, Achilles used the bruised raw fresh herb to staunch the blood of his warriors' wounds. Unfortunately, its healing properties could not save Achilles himself. That yarrow actually does have value in healing wounds is reflected in its many common names: "soldier's woundwort", "knight's millefollium", "herbe militaris", "bloodwort", and "staunchweed". Millefolium, meaning "thousand leaves" refers to yarrow's double-divided lacy leaves that look like little feathers.

In my garden I prefer to grow native California plants and some *Achilleas* meet that criterion. In fact, *Achilleas* are native to many parts of the world. *A. ageratifolia*, with its low mat of silvery leaves, is otherwise known as Greek yarrow and is native to the Balkan region. *A. taygetea*, a favorite for its dense clusters of bright yellow flowers, is native to the Levant, the eastern Mediterranean region which stretches across north Africa to the Middle East. *A. millefolium* or common yarrow is listed by several sources as a California native. However, it appears to be very widely spread across the United States, Canada and Europe and can claim native status in a number of locations.

Many colors of *Achilleas* have been developed as cultivars and hybrids. Of the six varieties of *Achillea* I have planted, 'Coronation

Gold' is my favorite. At the entrance of my garden path, its bright yellow blossoms on three-foot stems serve as welcoming candles.

Further down the path are pale yellow 'Moonshine' and 'Salmon Beauty' with pinkish blossoms. 'Paprika' has brick-red flowers. These varieties are later blooming than 'Coronation Gold', are about two feet tall and have relatively weaker stems.

Recently I planted *A. wilzeckii*, a short plant, less than 12 inches tall, with white flowers. In contrast to the tiny individual flowers in the flat-topped clusters typical of *Achilleas*, this one's individual flowers are much larger and each daisy-like blossom in the flat umbel is easily distinguished. The pure white flowers with yellow centers provide effective contrast in a low border mixed with the electric-blue flowers of perennial lobelia. The leaves of *A. wilzeckii* are dentate (tooth-like) rather than feathery and the plant grows in a low mound.

The final variety of *Achillea* in my garden is *A. borealis*, a pink yarrow from California's Channel Islands. In just a few weeks, the plants have grown from four inches tall in four-inch pots to fifteen-inch plants about to bloom. They have light green foliage in contrast to the grayish foliage of my other *Achilleas*.

Propagating plants in my garden always gives me great pleasure. When clumps of *Achillea* become crowded, they can and should be divided, thus providing a source of new plants. I have also observed that 'Coronation Gold' produces baby plants on its stems. If those stems are pinned to the ground with a wire hoop, the tiny plants will take root and grow. They can also be removed from the mother plant and rooted in potting soil. 'Moonshine', 'Salmon Beauty', and 'Paprika' behave differently. After blooming, the central plant dies down and a group of tiny plants appears the next season in a ring around the edge of the previous plant. These tiny sprouts will flourish if watered regularly, developing into a cluster of flowering plants. This self-propagating aspect of *Achilleas* is one reason I like them so much. I generally deadhead, that is, remove dead flowers, regularly, so my *Achilleas* do not have a chance to produce seed.

~ *Flowering Plants* ~

Achillea seed is available and, according to several sources, *Achilleas* may be employed as a lawn substitute. One can prepare the site as for a lawn, broadcast yarrow seeds in the spring, water, and eventually mow the plants several times a year. Once established, *Achilleas* are very drought tolerant, so these low-growing feathery leaves could produce a pleasing substitute for water-guzzling grass.

Achillea flowers are excellent for use in both fresh and dried flower arrangements. In order to preserve their color, dry the flowers in silica gel.

Achilleas have also made their way into the realm of philosophy. For centuries, the strong, straight stalks of yarrow have been dried and used by Chinese philosophers for throwing the I Ching.

To use *Achilleas* for their medicinal properties in infusions, they should be gathered while in bloom and dried in a warm room. According to tradition, an infusion of *Achillea*, made by pouring one pint of boiling water over one ounce of the dried herb, may be used as a regular hairwash to prevent baldness.

One final use of yarrow I find particularly charming. This is taken from *Stalking the Healthful Herbs* by Euell Gibbons:

> "Sew an ounce of the herb into a little flannel square and place it under your pillow. Before going to bed, recite,
>
> 'Thou pretty herb of Venus' tree,
> Thy true name is yarrow
>
> Now who my bosom friend must be,
> Pray tell thou me tomorrow.'
>
> If all has been properly done, just before you awaken the next morning, you will see your future husband or wife in a vision."

Not So Finicky Fuchsias

BY I'LEE HOOKER

Fuchsias are the perfect plant for any garden in the Bay area. The moisture from the summer fog that rolls over our coastline and through the Bay keeps them cool. The frost-free winters allow them to grow all year. They also work well a little further inland, if sheltered from the hot sun and dry hot winds and given a little frost protection.

The first fuchsia (*Fuchsia triphylla flore coccinea*) was discovered in what is now the Dominican Republic in the late seventeenth century and named after a German herbalist, Dr. Leonhart Fuchs. Fuchsiamania hit in England during the Victorian era, with nurserymen propagating and hybridizing fuchsias. Hunting expeditions fanned out across the world looking for new and different species. Enthusiasm died down in England at the advent of World War I, when people became more concerned with growing vegetables than ornamental plants. Fuchsias were rare in the United States until 1929, when the American Fuchsia Society was founded. A group of enthusiastic members, using European cultivars, began creating their own hybrids. Interest increased rapidly in the United States and again in England.

Fuchsias bloom in profusion with their characteristic vibrant colors ranging from magenta and purple to soft pink and white. The flashy hybridized fuchsias look like colorful dancers twirling in the wind, with sepals (outer part that flares back) of white red, pink or orange and corollas (inside part) that are almost any color except yellow and are often ruffled or double petals. They offer movement and color to the garden border and are charming in hanging baskets or topiaries in the patio. Hummingbirds find them most attractive.

~ *Flowering Plants* ~

So why aren't they a staple in our gardens? The fuchsia gall mite unfortunately is the answer. It arrived on some contraband fuchsias in Daly City around 1980, and has since naturalized in California. Most common fuchsia hybrids are cultivars bred from *Fuchsia magellanica*, which is from Chile and Venezuela. Unfortunately, the fuchsias from this part of South America are highly susceptible to the fuchsia mite. The fuchsia mite originated in Brazil, where the Brazilian fuchsias and their descendants are highly resistant to the gall mite.

Mites are tiny pests, which along with spiders and ticks, are members of the arachnid class and cannot be classified as insects. If the leaves of your fuchsia are curled and distorted, the fuchsia mite has infected your plant. They attack the new tender growth of the fuchsias. This mite is extremely difficult to completely eradicate. If you are determined to grow fuchsia plants, here are a few suggestions. Quarantine newly acquired fuchsias and observe them carefully for two to three weeks for any symptoms of galls. At the first sign of gall development, prune heavily. Fuchsia grower Barney Gonzalves of San Diego recommends spraying with a diluted solution of "Simple Green" (about one-half of one percent). Other nontoxic sprays like Neem oil, soap-alcohol mixtures or soap-horticultural oil mixtures may also be effective. Stay away from the more toxic pesticides because they are very harmful to hummingbirds, which are frequent visitors to fuchsias.

The Bay area is very lucky to have Strybing Arboretum breeding mite resistant fuchsias. By using a rare relative of *F. magellanica*, called *F. campos-portoi*, which is strongly resistant to the fuchsia gall mite, Strybing has been able to develop a new breeding line of fuchsias. They have the classic forms and flower types of traditional garden hybrid fuchsias, but do not develop galls when exposed to the fuchsia mite. Strybing is encouraging growers to acquire these species and cultivars and get them into the wholesale trade. The best place to see the new mite resistant hybrids and species fuchsias is the Fuchsia Dell in Golden Gate Park (near the Conservatory and Arguello Street entrance). Watch for these fuchsias at Strybing Arboretum and University of California at Berkeley Botanical Garden sales.

All nurseries sell fuchsias. Emphasize that you want only proven mite resistant fuchsias. Two common safe fuchsias offered in nurseries are *F. thymifolia*, an erect spreading shrub, with tiny pink or white flowers and *F. procumbens*, a prostrate spreading form with small unusual upright flowers. Two other species of fuchsias that are harder to find but well worth the effort are *F. boliviana* and *F. fulgens*. *F. boliviana*, variety 'Alba', is a large shrub or small tree which produces a cluster of flowers with white panicles about two inches long, terminating with a burst of small dark pink petals. *F. fulgens*, an arching upright shrub, has pale coral to scarlet pendants with lime green at the tips of the sepals. Don't let your local nursery talk you into buying 'Gartenmeister Bonstedt' as a mite resistant alternative fuchsia. It is a very attractive fuchsia with dark smoky colored leaves and clusters of bright pink-orange flowers. It looks like other fuchsias that are mite resistant, but it is very susceptible and can become severely galled if infested.

Here are two lists of mite resistant fuchsias from Strybing Arboretum. You might ask your nursery if they have them or if they can order them for you.

Fuchsia Species	Modern Hybrids
Fuchsia arborescens	*F.* 'Fanfare'
F. boliviana	*F.* 'Campo Thilco' (Strybing)
F. xbacillaris (aka "*F. thymifolia*")	*F.* 'Campo Molino' (Strybing)
F. denticulata	*F.* 'Miep Aalhuizen'
F. fulgens	*F.* 'Galfrey Blush' and
F. glazioviana	'Galfrey Lye' (Strybing)
F microphylla ssp. *aprica*	*F.* 'Campo Victrix' (Strybing)
F. paniculata	*F.* denticulata 'Fandent 12'
F. regia	*F.* 'Dainty Angels Earring'

Orchids for the Home

by Virginia Havel

Orchids are almost everyone's favorite indoor flowering plant, but, unfortunately, not everyone who tries has success growing them. Many of these hopeful growers fall in love with the fantastic colors and varieties of orchids they first see at orchid shows, and with high hopes come home with an exotic new plant. Sadly, expectations are soon dashed when the plant stops blooming and refuses to ever put out another flower. Eventually, a half-dead plant is discarded, and yet another defeated orchid grower is born.

This article provides some background on orchids and will point out some common problems the beginner may encounter. A short list of easy-to-grow varieties is included. By choosing the best kinds of orchids for your particular situation, you can vastly increase the odds of growing healthy flowering plants and you can have fun with your success.

The orchid family has the most species of all plant families—some thirty thousand worldwide. If you take into account all the new plants still being discovered and the hybrids and cultivars being developed, the number of varieties becomes almost infinite. Orchids grow in all continents except Antarctica. They are found at elevations from sea level to nine thousand feet. The greatest numbers occur in the tropics. Orchids are either terrestrial, growing in soil, or epiphytic, growing in trees. Epiphytic plants are not parasitic. Through air roots, they obtain their nutrient needs from rain-wash and wind-blown debris. Although the roots cling to trunks and branches, they do not penetrate the tree's bark. Tropical orchids have adapted to life in treetops because of the severe competition for light and space on the forest floor.

Although orchids differ greatly in size, shape, color, and specialized features, they all have the same basic anatomy. The flower parts consist of three sepals and three petals that may be indistinguishable, but usually one petal, the lip, is modified in various ways – color, shape, spots, stripes, or spurs. The male flower part, the anther, is fused with the female style and stigma to produce the column. Pollen from the anther forms a sticky mass called pollinia, which is transferred to another orchid by insects or birds.

Millions of seeds develop in the ovary. Seeds are minute and lack the stored food found in most plant seeds. Germination in nature usually requires partnership with a fungus that provides sufficient nutrition for the embryo to thrive. Commercially, orchids are grown from seed by germinating them on agar jelly plates containing nutrients. This technique vastly increases the number of orchids that can be raised in nurseries. Some nurseries also clone meristematic cells from the growing tips to make thousands of the best hybrids available at reasonable prices.

In the Bay area we have seven genera of native orchids, all of which are terrestrial. The tiny calypso orchid (*Calypso bulbosa*) lives in shady woods on the north side of Mount Tam. A rare ladyslipper (*Cypripedium californicum*) is found in moist canyons above Muir Woods. Papermill Creek and other streambeds are habitats for stream orchids (*Epipactis gigantea*). Bog orchids (*Platanthera*) and ladies' tresses (*Spiranthes*) grow in open meadows and bogs. Rattlesnake plantain (*Goodyera oblongifolia*) has dark green leaves with white veins and is found in shady woodlands. Only one genus (*Corallorhiza*) is a non-green (saprophytic) plant. It is pale with red stripes or spots and lives on organic matter in deep woodlands. Our beautiful native orchids deserve protection and should not be removed from the wild.

Some recommended orchids for beginners include *Cymbidiums*, *Phalaenopsis*, *Paphiopedilums* and *Cattleyas*. There are many other genera that can be tried if you understand their special needs.

Most problems growing orchids stem from extremes of heat and dryness. Orchids grow best in a warm, damp environment, and that

~ Flowering Plants ~

is not compatible with the Bay area's climate of cool wet winters and warm dry summers. Cymbidiums are adaptable to our outside conditions if protected from hot sun and chill (below 28°F). They produce multiple flowering stalks and can be found in many colors and sizes. Like all epiphytic orchids they should be planted in a special orchid medium such as bark.

Phalaenopsis, *Cattleya* and *Paphiopedilum* orchids are best in greenhouses, but can be grown outside in warm weather or in the home with good natural light (but not in direct sunlight). *Cattleyas* need more light than the others. Increased humidity is supplied by clumping plants together in a tray filled with wet gravel or clay pellets. Adding ferns and other plants increases the humidity. Water once a week by spraying in the morning on the roots, stems, and leaves, but not on flowers or buds. Feed regularly with any balanced fertilizer about once a month. In addition, good air circulation around plants and roots is necessary. In small, enclosed spaces, a fan may be helpful. When plant roots outgrow the container, replanting in new bark in a larger pot is recommended. Plants may stop blooming for a period after repotting, so don't do it more often than every two or three years.

Consider the Lily

~

BY VIRGINIA HAVEL

If you have been looking through the new garden catalogs, you are probably aware that the lily has become one of the most desirable flowers to grow. Now available in exotic colors and forms, lilies are breathtakingly beautiful with delightful fragrances. Easy to grow perennials, they have long lasting blossoms and make great cut flowers for the home. But beware. If you plant these appealing lilies, you may soon be hooked!

The name "lily" conjures up a vision of a very beautiful, fragrant flower. Historically the name referred to any lovely flower, and thus many plants called lilies are not in the lily family—for example, calla lily, water lily and canna lily. The old lily family is currently being divided into some forty new families as the result of new information from DNA analysis. Only seven genera are now in the proposed new lily family, including the genus, *Lilium*, the subject of this essay.

Lilies have flower parts in threes. Three sepals and three petals make up the perianth. Inside the perianth are the three-parted stigma (female) and six anthers (male) bearing the pollen. Insects find their way to the stigma by way of spots arranged on the inner side of the petals leading down to nectar glands. The flowers attached to the stem by a pedicel are either single or in clusters. The six leaves are in a whorl around the stem or arranged alternately. An underground fleshy bulb made of modified leaves, carries the plant through the winter season. Bulbs may divide to create more bulbs. Some species also reproduce by bulbils along the stem that fall to the ground and start new plants. Roots along the stem just below the ground and at the base of the bulb anchor the plant firmly in soil.

~ Flowering Plants ~

Lilies are native only to the northern hemisphere, mainly in temperate regions of Asia, Europe, and North America. About eighty native species are known worldwide, of which twelve grow in California. Many of these are considered rare and endangered. We have two species in the Bay area, *Lilium pardalinum* and *L. occidentale*.

References to lilies go back to ancient times, in the Bible and in Egyptian writings and art. Ancient peoples utilized lily bulbs as part of their staple diet, for animal fodder and as dyes and medicines. Lilies were a symbol for purity of the Virgin Mary in Christianity. During the Middle Ages, lilies were grown in monastery gardens for their beauty and used in religious ceremonies. In the seventeenth century, cultivation became increasingly important when the lily caught on as a highly desirable horticultural specimen. Plant collectors from Europe and America traveled to China and Japan in search of new varieties. The Japanese, in particular, developed a vast commercial empire, shipping lilies around the world. This period in history is known as the "Century of the Lily".

Lilies are suitable for almost any kind of landscape situation. They grow well in containers, in rock gardens, along fences and walls, as backdrops and as borders. Lilies can be found in many sizes from one to six feet tall. Some lilies will bloom for several weeks. Oriental lilies bloom late in the season after early bloomers finish.

The popularity of lilies is once again increasing because they bloom after other bulb flowers are through. They also require less sun than some other bulbs. Recommended are the Oriental hybrids, such as 'Stargazer' (rose-red with white margins), 'Casablanca' (pure white) and 'Acapulco' (pink). Other species that have been grown successfully locally are *L. regale and L. rubrum*.

Bulbs must always be kept moist and cool, and should be planted soon after purchase. Plant in well-drained, loose soil with organic matter. Clay soils need to be amended with compost and sand. Keep the roots cool and moist year-round. In warm locations, plant in filtered sun. Protect from deer and gophers, and control aphids.

CHAPTER EIGHT

*Other Plants
of Special Interest*

Landscaping with Ornamental Grasses

by Virginia Havel

The grass family includes many useful and diverse plants that grow in all parts of the world. In the past, grasses have been used in gardens mainly for lawns and turf, but more recently landscapers have discovered the unique advantages of incorporating both native and cultivated varieties of grasses into their horticultural designs.

Increased demands for attractive new grasses have resulted in a huge variety available in the nursery trade. The artist landscaper has become aware that the special qualities of grasses can create a mood of peace and serenity or a sense of oneness with nature in the garden. Grasses have provided a new dimension of experiencing the garden with all one's senses.

Perennial bunch grasses have lovely rounded shapes, surviving and replacing themselves for many years. Annual grasses re-seed year after year and are attractive when dry in the fall and winter. The blades and flowering stalks are soft tones of greens and blues, subtle mauves and rusts, gold and yellows. In the fall, tans and browns predominate. Variegated leaves accent some grass plants. The swaying of grasses in the breeze adds movement to the garden—a hypnotic rhythm like the ripples on a lake. And after the foliage dries and seeds ripen, the gentle rustling sounds enhance the visual effect.

Size and form of grass plants vary from tiny rock garden mounds to giant bamboo, suitable for shade and hedges. Grasses may be evergreen or ephemeral with persisting colorful dried flowers. Some grasses love a wet environment while others are drought tolerant. And many are deer resistant. There are grasses to fill the needs of all landscape requirements.

Grass gardens usually include sedges (*Cyperus*) and rushes (*Juncus*) from closely related families, and other plants with grass-like qualities: horsetails (*Equisetum*), cattails (*Typha*) and New Zealand flax (*Phormium*). Rushes have solid spike-like stems, and sedges often have umbrella-like arrangements of the inflorescence (flowers).

Some native grasses and sedges are excellent as ground covers. The best choices for lawn substitutes are evergreen plants, low growing, with dense foliage that can withstand traffic, and preferably require little water. Other ground cover grasses may be used for meadows. Grasses about eight to eighteen inches high, closely spaced and mixed with wildflowers or bulbs, are suitable for open areas of gardens. Some recommended species by *California Horticulture* magazine are *Carex pansa*, California meadow sedge, *C. dolichostachya* var. 'Kaga Nishidi', a Japanese variegated form, *C. morrowi*, a cream-edged cultivar called 'Ice Dance', and a California native, Berkeley sedge (*C. tumulicola.*). For a rock garden, grow mounded forms with their flower spikes in bloom at different seasons. Most alpine species will do well. Japanese gardens feature carefully selected rocks placed with colorful grasses such as blue gama (*Boutelua gracilis*), striped orchard grass (*Dactylis glomerata* 'Variegata'), most fescues, and annual and perennial fountain grasses.

Grasses and grass-like plants that require a wet habitat are attractive near a pond, fountain or natural seep. A sunken tub filled with rock and water is an easy way to create this wetland affect. Plant umbrella plant (*Cyperus alternifolius*), horsetail (*Equisetum hyemale*), bulrush (*Scripus cernuus*), and cattail (*Typha augustifolia*) in and around the pool. Incidentally, the reedy horsetail species, a Marin native, is very attractive as filler in cut floral arrangements.

Large showy plantings add focus and are sculptural showpieces in the garden. Pampas grass has long been popular, appreciated for its large white plumes. Unfortunately, it is no longer recommended due to its invasive nature. *Pennistamen* and *Miscanthus* cultivars of fountain grass, are noteworthy for their large cascading leaves and showy flowers. The flowers of Zebra grass (*Miscanthus sinensis*) last late into winter.

Lawns: Beauty and Beast

by Jan Specht

Q. What is lovely to look at, a high water user and very labor intensive?
A. A lawn.

Most lawns are either warm season grasses, which produce most of their growth during the summer and turn brown in winter, or cool season grasses that are green all year and produce most of their growth in spring and fall. Cool season grasses require more water than warm season grasses, but in general, lawns are water hogs—they use lots of water that the Bay area does not have and cannot afford. In addition to using lots of water, lawn fertilizers, pesticides and herbicides end up in our creeks and Bay from over watering and storm runoff.
    Lawns serve essentially two purposes. One is beauty and one is function. If a beautiful view is what you want, it can be accomplished with many other plants that use far less water and take less work. Ground covers vary in height from one-half inch to about four feet and there are many choices. Function implies how much foot traffic the lawn can tolerate and this limits the choices of what can be used in place of turf. Just as there are no perfect lawn grasses, there are no perfect plants to replace them. However, at least two do come close. Fescue (several types including a dwarf) uses about twenty-five percent less water; and a turf variety of buffalo grass uses about fifty percent less water. Both take foot traffic and are much lower maintenance than lawn grasses. Another way to conserve water is to simply reduce the size of the lawn. The size should fit the function. Ask yourself if you really need that (big) lawn.
    Lawns require a good deal of effort to look good. In California, an unhealthy lawn is more likely to be caused by poor lawn care or

planting the wrong type of lawn for the area than by insects. The following maintenance measures will produce a healthy lawn and conserve water, time and money.

Improper irrigation is the most common cause of lawn damage. Brown spots from uneven watering often occur because of poorly spaced or aligned sprinkler heads or unmatched heads. Correcting these problems will decrease water waste and improve the lawn. Water slowly to prevent runoff and water deeply. The soil should be wet about four inches down and should be checked immediately after irrigating. To check the moisture depth, push a garden spade into the turf and push it to one side or use a soil probe to remove a plug of grass and soil. This should be done in several different spots to avoid over watering in some areas and under watering in others. Too frequent watering promotes shallow roots. Wet spots waste water, weaken turf by causing poor soil aeration and fungal root diseases and allow invasion by shallow-rooted weeds. Dry spots cause poor growth and shallow roots that contribute to thatch and allow invasion by deep-rooted weeds. Check moisture levels again and water only when the soil is almost dry. It should be checked throughout the growing season since water requirements change depending on temperature. Establishing a water schedule without checking the water level in the soil usually results in excess watering.

Appropriate fertilizing is important for a healthy lawn. But over fertilizing is a waste of time and money, can pollute our creeks and Bay, encourages fungal disease and causes excessive growth with increased water needs. If you are unsure about your soil nutrients, have it professionally tested. Most warm season lawns in the Bay area require four to five pounds of nitrogen per one thousand square feet for the season. If you mow properly, the small pieces of grass clippings can be left on the lawn. They decompose rapidly, don't leave a mat, and provide nitrogen. If left on the lawn with each mowing, they will provide about half the annual nitrogen needs. A one-quarter inch layer of sifted compost in one thousand square feet will provide another pound. If compost is used, it must be free of any large pieces

~ *Other Plants of Special Interest* ~

and have the consistency of fine crumbly soil. Incompletely composted material risks having weed seeds, bad odor, flies or debris on the lawn. If you use a chemical fertilizer, look for a slow-release type.

Lawn mowing should only be done when the grass is dry. Mower blades must be kept sharp; otherwise the grass blades tear and are more susceptible to insects and disease. The actual grass height depends on the grass species. Never mow lower than one-third of the grass blade height for several reasons. This small amount allows one to use the clippings as fertilizer. Deeper cuts mean less photosynthesis, so roots will not be healthy and fewer nutrients can be absorbed. This also exposes too much of the grass to the hot sun, allows weed seeds to establish and encourages pest and disease problems. Using the one-third rule means the lawn will have to be cut more often (about every five days) when it is growing faster early in the season but less often when it is growing slower.

Thatch is an accumulation of dead and dying grass roots and stems that accumulate above the soil but below the grass blade. Some grass species produce more thatch than others, but improper watering and over fertilizing also contribute to thatch. It causes a mat that prevents water, air and fertilizer from reaching the soil. Moisture in the thatch also contributes to pest and disease problems. A significant amount of live grass roots may be trying to grow in the thatch. A thin layer of thatch (one-quarter to one-half inch) can be good because it insulates soil temperature and can reduce compaction from some foot traffic. If you can't poke a finger through the grass into the soil, the thatch is probably over one-half inch thick and is a problem. Thatch can be removed any time but the best time is spring when growth is faster and can fill the bare spots before the weeds move in. Various mechanical de-thatching devices can be purchased or rented. If compost is used on a regular basis for fertilizing, it can help decompose some thatch because it contains millions of beneficial microorganisms. Use of toxic pesticides will kill these beneficial microbes.

If your lawn has areas of heavy foot traffic, brown spots, water pooling or grass thinning, soil compaction could be the problem.

Alternate the mowing pattern to prevent compaction from the mower. If you can't push a screwdriver five to six inches into the soil, it is compacted. Irrigate so the soil is moist five to six inches down before using an aerator to correct the problem. Nutrients, water and air cannot penetrate compacted soil.

A weed-free lawn is impossible, but a dense, vigorous lawn can out compete many weeds. Decide how many you can tolerate, since even a fair number of weeds are not easily visible. Protect yourself, anyone who uses the lawn and the environment by avoiding herbicides and digging weeds by hand. Fill in bare spots with grass seed to prevent more weeds. Corn gluten is safe to use and kills weed seeds before they emerge. It also kills grass seeds so it can be used only on established lawns. Corn gluten contains nitrogen, so be sure to factor this in when fertilizing.

Insecticides should never be applied unless the insect is identified. Such caution will also preserve common beneficial lawn organisms like predatory ants, some beetles, springtails and millipedes. If you have brown spots in the lawn and have ruled out cultural problems as well as dog urine as the culprit, you may try the pyrethrum test to detect cutworms, sod webworms, chinch bugs, fiery skipper larvae and billbug adults. Mix one tablespoon of this least toxic insecticide containing 1-2% pyrethrins in one gallon of water in a sprinkling can and apply to one square yard of turf. The solution irritates the insects and within ten minutes they come to the surface where they can be captured. If you cannot identify the insect, take it to your local Master Gardeners' office. This test will not detect white grubs, which feed on grass roots. Roll a section of lawn back and look for whitish C-shaped grubs up to one and one-half inches long with six legs and a reddish head. Least toxic treatments are available for most of these pests, but all must be used at the right time to be effective.

Ground Covers

by Jan Specht

Ground covers are very versatile plants. Definitions vary, but many people include plants that range from less than one inch tall up to three to four feet tall. Others define ground covers as a bed of low growing, spreading or multiplying plants. Any plant that spreads and isn't too tall can be used as a ground cover as long as it looks attractive.

Ground covers are great problem solvers in the garden. Many spread quickly to carpet bare spots, including dry soil under trees. The low growing, spreading kinds can cover a hillside or other areas that are not easily accessible. Any homeowner who has planted a steep slope knows how physically difficult it is and wants plants that require little maintenance. Hillside situations also require deep-rooted ground covers that provide erosion control to stabilize the slope. Densely growing, established ground covers decrease maintnence by covering so well that weeds can't grow and mulching isn't needed because there is no exposed ground. The need for fertilizer is reduced because the natural breakdown of flowers, berries and leaves produces humus that releases plant nutrients back to the soil. This decreases the work and the cost of gardening. Also, they can cover the ground while bulbs are growing and, depending on their height, can hide dying bulb foliage, too.

Rapid growers will fill in areas quickly and drought tolerant ones can greatly decrease water use. Shallow rooted ground covers planted under trees and shrubs break up the soil, thereby increasing porosity and nutrients for the taller plants. It is preferable to use drought tolerant ground covers instead of large areas of concrete, rocks or stones. Plants use carbon dioxide and give oxygen back to the atmosphere. Stones don't.

Some ground covers can provide fire retardant protection, while others are frost tolerant and many look attractive mixed with favorite annuals. Ground covers do not tolerate much foot traffic so if you need a path in the area, use stepping stones.

There is a very large variety of ground covers, each of which can provide all or some of the above benefits. They can be perennials, wildflowers, ornamental grasses, low shrubs, herbs, vines, or bulbs. Some can supply year around interest with flowers, berries, attractive seed heads or foliage. In addition, they may be clumping or sprawling, deciduous or evergreen, and with foliage of various colors or textures. A mixture of different kinds of ground covers is preferable to a single kind. A monoculture is never good because if there is a disease or insect problem, it could destroy the entire area. Also, diverse plants support diverse types of beneficial organisms, which are necessary for a healthy garden.

The best time to put new plants in the garden is fall because the cool wet season allows plants to develop a deep, more extensive root system. During spring and summer the plant energy goes into producing stem, leaf, flower, fruit or seed instead of root development. In general, three months is an adequate period for root establishment. Drought tolerant plants will still require summer water the first year but in subsequent years will be truly water conserving.

When looking for ground covers, don't be overwhelmed by choices. Carefully assess your site and follow the cardinal rule of gardening: the right plant in the right place. A plant that requires full sun probably won't do well in light shade. Find out how large the plant is at maturity and don't use it if it becomes larger than you'd like. Be clear on the water requirements and use plants that are known to thrive in your garden zone. It is also preferable to buy the smaller plants (one gallon instead of five gallon size) whenever possible because the younger plant produces a deeper, more widespread root system at maturity, enabling it to better survive drought conditions and other stresses. An exception to this would be some slow growing plants when it is important to fill in an area sooner than later.

Plants for Clay Soil

~

by Barbara J. Euser

California live oaks (*Quercus agrifolia*) and valley oaks (*Q. lobata*) live happily in clay soil. But what is good for oaks presents a challenge to many plants: it is difficult for plants to extend their roots through the tiny, densely packed particles. Water molecules get stuck, retained for much longer in clay than they are in sandy soil. Air has a tough time penetrating, too. What can a gardener do?

One solution is to change the character of the soil in the garden by amending it with either organic or inorganic materials. Another solution is to choose plants for the garden that are naturally adapted to clay soils.

My hillside garden is dominated by a live oak tree. The soil throughout my garden is clay. I have chosen plants that are adapted to the existing soil. However, I am also mulching liberally with shredded bark each year. I find that, year by year, as the mulch breaks down, it adds a new layer to the soil. By mulching, I am gradually changing the character of the clay soil. In the meantime, several species of native California plants have proven especially successful in my garden.

Salvia clevelandii is one of my favorites. I first encountered it on a hike near Muir Beach. In the warm afternoon sun, the unmistakable fragrance of the leaves perfumed the air. The bushes were thriving along the roadside. Their whorled lavender-colored blossoms encircled the long stems like delicate rings. What a plus to discover that the bushes I bought at the nursery thrive in clay soil!

Another native that I met on the open slopes of Mt. Tam, sticky monkey flower (*Mimulus aurantiacus*), also grows well in clay soil. Bright orange flowers peek out of the dark green foliage of these bushes in the spring. I have planted several of these in my lower garden where they please me year after year. The common monkey flower (*M. guttatus*) likes clay soil, too.

The feathery silver foliage of sandhill sage (*Artemesia pyncocephala*) brightens the edge of the path down my hill. *Artemesia*s prefer full sun. Their rounded forms contrast with the stiff upright fans of African iris, also called fortnight lilies (*Dietes*) growing nearby. Although fortnight lilies are reputed to require fairly good soil, they have naturalized bountifully in my clay soil.

California wild lilacs (*Ceanothus*) tolerate clay soil and generally harsh conditions. In the wild, they grow on rocky slopes and go without surface water all summer. In the garden, their biggest enemy is too much water, which can cause root rot. I have planted two varieties of *Ceanothus* in the clay soil under my oaks: Carmel Creeper (*C. griseus horizontalis*) and one other, discovered on the grounds of the Hearst Castle, *C. hearstiorum*. Both have purple blossoms in the spring. I find the shiny, round green foliage of Carmel Creeper particularly appealing.

In addition to these shrubs, I have a number of native herbaceous perennials that do well in clay soil. These include the plants I think of as the *Sisyrinchium* sisters, blue-eyed grass (*S. bellum*) and yellow-eyed grass (*S. californicum*). Unfortunately, when I planted them, I didn't realize that although blue-eyed grass does well in dry areas, yellow-eyed grass prefers wetter places. Half my yellow-eyed grass perished for lack of water.

In a sunny section of my garden, common thrift (*Armeria maritima*) grows well enough in the clay soil, however, I have read that *Armeria* require excellent soil drainage. If that is the case, the very nature of clay soil, to trap water and hold it, may explain why my thrift is not truly thriving.

Various yarrows (*Achilleas*) are very tolerant of clay soil. These sun-loving plants are some of my favorites for their wide range of flower color and many medicinal properties. In an essay I devoted entirely to Achilleas, I failed to mention one memorable event in my family's lore. My parents and I were camping in the Colorado Rockies

~ *Other Plants of Special Interest* ~

when my father developed an excruciating toothache. We were many miles from a dentist. It would be a full day before we could get to one. My father packed a wad of yarrow leaves around his tooth. It stopped hurting. Not only that, the effect lasted twenty-four hours. He has never forgotten the experience, although when I wrote my essay on *Achilleas*, I apparently had. Now the story is told.

Finally, another Southwest native that is doing very well in my clay soil is *Gaura*, (*G. lindheimeri*). I have heard this plant called "butterflies-in-the-wind" and that is just what it looks like. One inch long white and pink blossoms open on long, nearly invisible stems above a mound of long green leaves. The blossoms appear to be floating and dancing in the breeze. The plants prefer full sun and continue blooming all summer. *Gaura* is reputed to self-seed. I anxiously anticipate this development.

When planting, especially in clay soil, it is important to avoid injury to the roots of plants. Soil should not be compacted too tightly around them. Water should not collect around the base of the plant. If planting near oak trees, respect the needs of the oak. Don't plant within six feet of the trunk of the oak, and then plant only species that don't require much irrigation.

There are many native California plants adapted to clay soils. This small sampling shows that by choosing the right plants, you can garden successfully in clay.

Cacti and Succulents

by Virginia Havel

Have you been looking for plants for your home or garden that thrive on neglect? If you have the kind of life style that most of us live today—rushing from one thing to another, often being away from home for days, frequently forgetting to water your house plants or your garden—then succulents and cacti may be just the right choices for you. These plants require less care than most because they tolerate drought, survive in overheated or air-conditioned homes and outside in shade and sun. Some species are even able to withstand frost. They aren't too picky about their soil either, but do need good drainage. An added bonus is the showy colorful flowers that cacti produce.

Members of the cactus family, cactacea, can be recognized by the presence of round pads called areoles on the stems and branches. All cacti store water in their leaves (when present), stems or roots, and thus all are succulents. This adaptation evolved for survival during periodic drought. In geological times, the earth's climate changed, becoming drier as the mountains were pushed up to create rain shadows and deserts. Other plant families adapted similarly to these conditions, and there are thousands of succulent species. Some of these mimic cacti almost exactly in shape, form, and spines, but because they lack areoles, they are not cacti. For example, there are also succulents in the lily, portulaca, goosefoot, iceplant (Aizonacea), mint and euphorbia plant families.

Cacti originated in the Americas and are found from Canada to Chile. Some species may have naturalized very early in Europe and Africa after the beginning of human civilization and are now widespread in the Mediterranean region. Cacti grow in deserts, coastal scrub, high glacial regions of the Sierra, coniferous forests and in dry

~ *Other Plants of Special Interest* ~

and wet tropics of South America. There are about two thousand species worldwide and twenty-seven species in California, but none are native to the Bay area.

Succulents are widespread in many different habitats of the world: high mountains, rocky cliffs, desert and salt marshes. Succulence is an adaptive response to drought, rapid drainage in rocky and sandy soil, high evaporation in windy, hot environments, and in salty or alkaline habitats. There are probably more than five thousand species worldwide.

The growing requirements for cacti and succulents are the same, so the following cultivation methods apply to both groups. Light is very important and most species need a minimum of four hours a day of sunlight. Greenhouses are perfect environments with weather protection, controlled humidity and light, but windowsills inside the home, particularly south-facing, are great for miniature deserts in shallow containers. Only snake plants (*Sanseviera*) seem to thrive in north-facing exposures. Cactus potting soil is rich in humus and contains perlite or vermiculite. Regular bagged potting soil with these additions also is suitable for container plants. The main thing to remember is good drainage and minimal watering to prevent root rot. Water as needed. This is dependent on the size and shape of the pot; type of container, whether ceramic, glazed, or plastic; location, for example greenhouse or garden; and exposure to sun and wind. Feed with a liquid fertilizer about three times a year during the growing season. In winter, water less frequently and stop feeding.

I never knew there were so many kinds of succulents until I visited the Great Petaluma Desert nursery. Jerry Wright, the owner, is a walking encyclopedia of knowledge about these plants. He has been in this location in Petaluma for over twenty years. Now he is phasing out the cultivation of ordinary small cacti and succulents and moving into the business of growing the unusual and rare succulent plants of the world. He plans to cater exclusively to collectors and botanical gardens. His rare plants come from many regions where he travels to collect and buy prize specimens. His greenhouses are filled with tiny miniatures to giant tree succulents. There are the lithrops, stone-like plants barely showing above the soil, in round and angular rock shapes, snakelike crawling specimens, barrel forms, rosettes, spiny dangerous-looking monstrosities, and more.

Perhaps the best part of the show is the many varieties of bonsai succulents. This is the new rage in container plants, according to Wright. Many are caudiciform (meaning tree-trunk form). The swollen trunk flares out at the base and supports a small leafy top. The base can be an enlarged stem, root, bulb, rhizome or corm. The plants may be upright, leaning or lying on the ground. Once you see these charming arrangements, you will want to grow one of your own. What an outlet for the artist in everyone to create such a combination of unique living material with a special container, selected rocks, gravel and driftwood! Bonsai succulents have the charm of conventional Japanese bonsai plants, but do not have to be ancient to achieve their great beauty.

Landscaping with Ferns

by Virginia Havel

Why would anyone want to plant ferns—a plant that never has flowers or fruit? Yet, ferns have been used since Victorian times as important accents in the parlor and conservatory, where their lacy delicate leaves add a feeling of softness and serenity. Despite the fact that ferns are not colorful or productive, they do have some special attributes.

Ferns come in many sizes and forms. You can use small filmy ferns in intimate rock gardens or huge tree ferns for shade and screening. Ferns are natural choices around rocks and water. Many kinds are drought-resistant and thrive in shade or sun. Although most species of ferns are tropical, some are adapted to temperate and alpine climates. Above all, ferns are easy to grow, resistant to pests and disease and require little maintenance.

Ferns and their allies are ancient plants that probably evolved from green algae. Although they were not the first plants to survive on land, ferns developed several adaptations that allowed them to increase in size and complexity, and to become less dependent on a watery environment. The outside cellular layer or "skin" became thickened and resistant to drying. Rhizomes and roots evolved for water and nutrient uptake into a vascular system through the stems into the leaves. Leaves were also a new modification for more efficient photosynthesis. All of these adaptations allowed ferns to become dominant among land plants of the Carboniferous Era. Fossilization of the gigantic fern forests of this period is the source of oil and coal deposits on which we now depend.

Fern reproduction has sexual and asexual phases, called alternation of generations by botanists. Both phases are dependent on water. The asexual phase begins with the release of spores from brown spots, called sori, on the underside of the fronds. The spores germinate on damp soil and grow into a small flat heart-shaped plant called a prothallus. These are inconspicuous, but are the site of sexual reproduction. Here microscopic sex organs produce eggs and sperms. It may be surprising to learn that ferns have free-swimming sperm cells that must move through water droplets to reach the egg cells and initiate the new fern. The new fern, growing out of the prothallus, may be discovered in moist places.

The basic structure of ferns includes a rhizome (underground stem) and leaves called fronds. Fronds arise from the rhizome and begin as tightly coiled buds that gradually uncoil to become the body of the fern. Young coiled leaves are known as "fiddleheads", and are prized by some as food delicacies. Fronds are usually divided into leaflets called pinnae, somewhat like feathers.

Ferns are found in all plant communities of the Bay area except salt marshes and sand dunes. There are twenty-three species divided among twelve genera. Some native ferns require special soils and high humidity, but others are quite suitable for Bay area gardens:

- Sword fern (*Polystichum munitum*) is excellent for many purposes. Its dark green, leathery foliage makes it drought-resistant and suitable for all day sun. It blends with other plants, is easy to grow and looks good throughout the year.
- Lady fern (*Athyriium felix-femina*), up to four feet tall, is very graceful. It adds a delicate touch but is somewhat fragile. Although is dies back in winter, it recovers in the early spring. It is easy to grow and will spread rapidly but needs ample watering.
- Giant chain fern, (*Woodwardia fiimbriata*) is our largest fern, growing up to six feet. The beautifully arranged pinnae give a chain-like appearance. It requires quite a lot of watering as its habitat is streams and seeps.
- Deer fern (*Blechnum spicant*) is an attractive fern, not more than one foot high. It is very well suited around ponds and fountains.

CHAPTER NINE

Trees and Underplantings

Caring for Our Majestic Oaks

by Diane Lynch

We are blessed with beautiful oaks in the Bay area. Oaks date back about ten million years and can live to be three hundred and fifty years old. Despite the problems with disease that have killed many trees, oaks remain and will continue to be an important landscaping element for Bay area gardens. The downside is that oaks are dying at a faster rate than they are being replaced. Studies have indicated that oaks in undisturbed lands are not regenerating at the same rate that they did before the 1850s and that decline has become particularly dramatic in the past couple of years with beetle and fungal infestations. Here are some guidelines to observe when landscaping around oaks, which can help ensure their survival and long life.

Lawns and oaks don't mix well in California. Oaks like to be dry in the summer and lawns require more water than almost any other plant. You can try to have some of both by letting the lawn go dry in the summer months out to the tree's drip line. If this does not appeal to you, consider redesigning the landscape and irrigation system to prevent any water from getting on the trunk and on the soil at least ten feet from the trunk, as this is a critical area for fungal root diseases. The area within the drip line should be as sparsely planted and undisturbed as possible. The fallen leaves can serve as mulch and nourish the soil, but keep them and any mulch away from the root crown or flare at the base of the trunk. Stressed or weakened oaks should be evaluated by a certified arborist or consulting horticulturist to determine the best treatment. In general, healthy trees do not need fertilizing.

We are so protective of our views that we often prune oaks excessively. This can limit the tree's ability to make food and thus weaken it. Oak trees are very sensitive to grade changes since most roots are within the top twelve inches. If you lower the grade, you remove roots and if you raise the grade, you cut off oxygen, nutrients and water to the tree. Paving, soil compaction (imagine how well you could breathe if a large person sat on your chest) from construction and increased water are also detrimental. While we used to recommend no summer water for oaks, the University of California now recommends summer watering at or slightly beyond the drip line to a depth of about eighteen inches every six weeks during the dry months.

Keep in mind that heavy planting, such as shrubs and groundcover, competes with the oak for nutrients and water. However, if you decide to plant under your oak trees, think native plants. By planting natives (and appropriate drought tolerant plants) you can feed the birds, hummingbirds and butterflies, as well as beautify your garden without sacrificing the oaks. Follow the distance guidelines above and, if space permits, start planting only at the drip line. Give consideration to the following plants:

SHRUBS

Natives that attract birds and work well around oaks include California lilac (*Ceanothus* spp.), elderberry (*Sambucus* spp.), Oregon grape (*Mahonia aquifolium*), Pacific wax myrtle (*Myrica californica*), manzanita (*Arctostaphyllos* spp.), California wild rose (*Rosa californica*), coffeeberry (*Rhamnus californica*), as well as currant/gooseberry (*Ribes* spp.). Butterflies are attracted to native coffeeberry and ceanothus. Hummingbirds like *Salvias* (*S. clevelandii* is a native), and *Grevillea* spp. Some of these shrubs get quite large and are best suited to growing outside the drip line.

GROUNDCOVERS

Remember to keep these and all plantings away from the crown. Hummingbirds and butterflies are attracted to Australian fuchsia (*Correa* spp.) as well as the native California fuchsia (*Epilobium* formerly

Zauscherinia californica). Birds like creeping mahonia (*Mahonia repens*), a native with blue berries. Emerald Carpet *Arctostaphyllos* and *A. uva-ursi* are dependable on banks.

Perennials

Wooly yarrow (*Achillea tomentosa* or *millefolium*) forms a mat of fernlike green leaves, which can be mowed to three inches. Day lily (*Hemerocallis* spp.) and *Iris douglasiana*, the native, as well as hybrids need little water. Coral bells (*Heuchera* spp.) and *Penstemon heterophyllus purdyi*, a native, and other cultivars attract hummers. *Santolina* is drought tolerant and Matilija poppy or fried egg plant (*Romneya coulteri*) is a stunning native that grows to eight feet. Pincushion flower (*Scabiosa*), Peruvian lily (*Alstroemeria* spp.) and western sword fern (*Polystichum munitum*) all require little water.

Grasses

Ask your nursery if non-native grasses are sterile so they don't seed themselves rampantly and become pests. Native bunch grasses occur under oaks, require little water and maintenance. They can be beautifully used as specimen plants or grouped to simulate a meadow. Natives to consider: melic grass (*Melica imperfecta*), deergrass (*Muhlenbergia rigens*), purple needlegrass, state grass of California (*Stipa pulchra*), *S. cernua, S. lepida, Bromus carinatus, Elymus tritiocoides,* tufted hairgrass (*Deschampsia caespitosa*), blue wild rye (*Elymus glaucus*).

Planting Under Oaks

by Barbara J. Euser

In the lower section of my sloping yard are three California live oak trees. One is old and venerable, the other two much younger. It is a section of our yard I have contemplated landscaping for several years. Last month railroad tie steps were built to make the area accessible. An area was scraped and flattened for a garden bench. The loveliest feature of this garden section is the old oak tree. The challenge was to find plants that could fill the bare dirt around it without endangering its health. Coast live oaks flourish in our cool wet winters and warm dry summers. Over watering is a serious health hazard. Oaks may develop crown root rot and oak root rot, soil-borne diseases fostered by moisture and warm temperatures. Understanding that, there are many native California plants and others that can thrive in the light shade and dry soil at the base of an oak.

For ground cover on our garden slope, I chose the low-growing *Ceanothus*, *C. hearstiorum*, which spreads in a star-like configuration and has tiny dark green leaves. Its spring flowers are medium blue— the small shapely cones of the wild lilac. This ceanothus was discovered on the grounds of Hearst Castle in southern California. I was told it is considered a rare and endangered species. The chance to plant and possess my own reputed rare and endangered California native intrigued me. I planted five. In two or three years, they will cover their allotted space. Ceanothus are also susceptible to root rot if over watered. They often grow naturally on rocky slopes and go without water all summer long. This makes them perfect partners for oaks. I will carefully water mine this first summer until they are established.

I planted another California native, island alum root, not far away. This heuchera (*Heuchera maxima*) is reputed to grow up to two feet across—one nursery told me three! Its flowers consist of hundreds of tiny coral bells hovering on thin stems above its large roundish leaves. This native of the Channel Islands is new to my garden and I am already imagining its eventual glorious size.

Douglas iris (*Iris douglasiana*) and the Pacific Coast Hybrid iris (*I.* 'PCH') in their lovely pale colors will provide more spring color. Their long pointed leaves contrast with the texture of the large heuchera leaves and the tiny dark green leaves of the ceanothus.

For a more delicate ground cover under the oaks, I could have chosen wood strawberries (*Fragaria californica*). These tough natives spread by runners that grow in all directions, eventually forming a mat difficult for weeds to invade. Birds find their seedy fruit delicious. Monkey flower bushes (*Mimulus aurantiacus*) flower during the spring and summer. Their funnel-shaped blossoms have two lips said to resemble a monkey's grinning face. Three I bought at the California Native Plant Society's plant sale in the fall were just beginning to bloom in May. The first to bloom this spring is cream-colored. The bushes with orange and bronze flowers will bloom later on.

To add summer color under the oaks, I planted three non-native species. These gave me particular pleasure because I was able to obtain them by dividing mature plants from other parts of my garden. Along the fence, I planted a row of bronze daylilies (*Hemerocallus*). They are very hardy with a long blooming season. Among the ceanothus, I planted several dwarf yellow daylilies whose height is in keeping with the low growing ground cover. Along the path, still shaded by the oaks, I planted summer-blooming red hot pokers (*Kniphofia uvaria*). Hummingbirds are attracted to the bright tubular flowers. The graceful arching leaves of all these plants are a pleasure even when they are not in bloom. Along a two-railroad-tie-high wall, I planted four rosemary bushes of the prostratus type (*Rosmarinus* 'Huntington Blue'). Although they grow only eighteen inches high, they will trail over the wall, becoming a gray-green curtain with tiny pale blue flowers. The flowers attract both birds and bees, and I often clip fresh sprigs of rosemary to use as a bed under salmon I am

~ *Trees and Underplantings* ~

grilling. Rosemary is a Mediterranean native that endures hot sun, poor soil, and requires no irrigation.

Other non-natives in my garden that would also do well under oaks include catmint (*Nepeta faassenii*) with its gray-green foliage and delicate purple flower spikes; Santa Barbara daisy (*Erigeron karvinskianus*) with its summer-long white flowers on dark mounds of foliage; lavender cotton (*Santolina chamaecyparissus*), a silver gray hill of foliage with bright yellow flowers in late spring; grevillea (*Grevillea rosmarinifolia*) with its needle-like green foliage and intricate rose and cream winter blossoms; various yarrows (*Achillea*) with gray or green foliage, depending on the variety, and tight flower umbels of white, yellow, salmon or brick (some *Achillea* are native Californians, others not).

To respect the oak, plants should not be placed too close to the trunk—six to ten feet is close enough. All of the plants mentioned are drought tolerant, but they must be irrigated during the first year to become established. To grow plants successfully under oaks, minimize disturbance of the oaks' root zone, minimize soil movement, and carefully target the root systems of the new plants when watering. With some thought and care, under oaks a lovely garden can bloom.

Sudden Oak Death Update

COMPILED BY DIANE LYNCH
FROM MATERIAL BY PAVEL SVIHRA, KIM KEIRNAN, NICOLE PALKOVSKY, BRUCE HAGEN, GAREY SLAUGTER, ANDREW STORER, MAGGI KELLY

There has been a great deal of press in the past year about Sudden Oak Death (SOD). The disease appears to be spreading, as cases have been identified in ten coastal counties. The species susceptible to SOD continue to increase and we now know that the tanbark oak, the first species identified with SOD, as well as the coast live oak, black oak, Shreve oak, rhododendron, huckleberry, California bay laurel, madrone, California buckeye and arrowwood (*Viburnum bodnatense*) , big leaf maple, manzanita, coffeeberry, toyon and hairy honeysuckle can all get SOD. Although SOD is fatal to oaks, it does not usually kill the non-oak plants mentioned above. Another concern is that areas with large numbers of dead and dying oaks are highly susceptible to fire, with late summer and fall being the most risky time of year.

Looking back in history, the American chestnut became almost extinct as a result of the fungus brought into New York on Asian nursery stock about 1900. Dutch elm disease, another fungal disease from Asia, was introduced in the 1920s and has eliminated most of the majestic elms across the United States. One wonders if SOD will cause the landscape of California to change dramatically.

What is Sudden Oak Death?

SOD is a disease caused by a previously unknown species of *Phytophthora ramorum*, a fungus-like organism that has killed many oaks and tanoaks in central coastal California. The name derives from the rapid decline and change of leaf color from green to brown. It is not currently known how SOD is spread. It is possible that some of the other species mentioned above may act as hosts and allow the spores of *P. ramorum* to build up to favorable levels for transmission to oaks.

Single or small stands of oaks in a garden setting are less likely to be infected with SOD than oaks on large properties, or those abutting parks or woodland open spaces.

What Symptoms Presage SOD?

- eark, viscous substance bleeding near the tree base
- reddish or tan-white dust resulting from bark and ambrosia beetles tunneling into the bark and wood of the tree
- appearance of dome-shaped fruiting bodies of *Hypoxylon* fungus, which are initially green, later turning black

The beetle boring dust and *Hypoxylon* fruiting bodies are secondary symptoms, which can occur on trees without Sudden Oak Death. To confirm whether or not oaks are infected with *P. ramorum*, contact your local University of California Cooperative Extension or County Agricultural Commissioner's office for current information about sampling.

How Can I Prevent SOD in My Trees?

Focus on maintaining oak health through proper cultural practices. Avoid disturbing roots (which can extend out past the drip line), prevent frequent irrigation, don't plant a lawn under native oaks, and minimize injuries to the trunk and lower limbs. Prune coast live oaks and black oaks during the dry summer months when the beetles and SOD pathogen are least active. Limit pruning to dead, dying and damaged branches.

Unless there is a nutrient deficiency proven by a soil test, there is no need to fertilize oak trees. Yellowing foliage on oaks or nearby plants could indicate a nutrient deficiency.

Recent newspaper articles have mentioned the use of the pesticide Astro as well as the fertilizer phosphonate used as a fungicide. Astro will not prevent *Phytophthora* infection but it will prevent secondary beetle attack. It is only effective in the spring, March and April, and the fall, August and September, when the beetles are active. It should be applied by a licensed pesticide applicator and you need to be aware that is has adverse environmental effects on bees and aquatic organisms. Those living near the Bay need to be wary of adding toxins to our Bay. Phosphonate cannot be legally used as a fungicide to treat SOD; it is registered as a fertilizer only.

What If My Tree Has Died from SOD?

Dead and dying trees should be removed as soon as possible to prevent damage to people or property. When the tree is cut down, leave the wood on the site. Split it for firewood, grind branches and use chips on site for mulch. Put wood and chips in a sunny area to promote rapid drying. If it cannot be used on site, contact the County Agriculture Commissioner's office for a transport permit. There are currently ten infected counties: Marin, Santa Cruz, Sonoma, Napa, San Mateo, Santa Clara, Monterey, and Mendocino, Alameda and Solano.

The Joy of Japanese Maples

by Maggie Agro

If you've longed for a graceful Japanese maple, but didn't feel you knew enough about them to make the serious investment they require, think again. For all of their grace and delicacy, they are as hardy and versatile as most shrubs and trees in your landscape.

The real joy in Japanese maples is choosing one that's perfect for you. Japanese maples are available in sizes from the true dwarf, starting at twelve inches, to the striking cascading forms and lower-growing forms, to uprights that grow to thirty-seven feet. They can be mixed in shade groupings or set apart as accents. And the selection of colors and leaf varieties is endless–every possible shade of green, gold, rust and burgundy with variegated or spotted leaves, lacy or divided or thread shaped, or with stems and tips in complimentary colors, with some who put on the best show in spring and others in fall.

But don't run out to your corner nursery to look–you'll only see a few. Take a short drive to Kenwood and visit Wildwood Farms, an independent family-run nursery spread over three and one-half acres with over three hundred varieties and five thousand trees.

I had all of the usual questions and Ricardo Monte, co-owner with his wife Sara, had surprising answers. What did I need to know to make an intelligent purchase? Depends on how you use it and what color and leaf shape you like; how big you want it to grow and what shape tree works best in your garden. Only ten out of three hundred must have shade and the rest can go anywhere. They can stand temperatures to 110°F if watered properly. They can grow in almost any climate.

If that doesn't sound simple enough, they are easy to plant and have shallow, fibrous root systems that make them perfect for areas near patios and curbs because they will not lift sidewalks. They are not competitive with other shrubs and make excellent companion plants. Their only critical need is regular, even watering of an average amount with good drainage. Proper water management is more important than soil or fertilizer. They make excellent container plants because those fibrous roots keep them from becoming pot bound too quickly and an evenly watered pot provides good drainage.

Wildwood propagates their maples through grafting which makes for a hardier mature plant that is more disease and mildew resistant. Grafting is the most common means of propagation for Japanese maples. After grafting, maples are usually held from two to five years, first in a greenhouse, then shade, and in increasing exposure times to "outside" air and temperature before they are "hardened off" for transplanting outside. Maples require much care and attention until they reach the market stage. It's this initial process that makes them pricier than most plants.

An excellent three-foot by three-foot specimen with a delicate spreading shape may have taken ten years of care and pruning to reach that stage of desirability and you can expect to pay a price relative to the amount of time and care invested. When you buy from a nurseryman who can explain his care for this plant over many years and who understands the work it takes to attain this cultivated beauty, you will develop a sense of wonder and custodianship for your plant.

A younger tree is more affordable, but will need pruning over several years to attain a graceful shape. It will probably do best in a container for a few years before transplanting it into the ground. If you plan on keeping it as a container plant, plan on top and root pruning every three to five years. Look for a healthy, vigorous plant and use any good potting soil. While container plants need fertilizer more than in-ground plants, ask your nurseryman about the best type for your particular species. And, when in doubt, less is better.

I can't wait to go back. I've already found the spot. Now, deciding on which lovely maple to bring home will be the real challenge!

Native Plants Under Redwoods

by Virginia Havel

You have probably heard that nothing grows under redwood trees. If you visit a redwood forest such as Muir Woods, you can easily observe that this is not true. I recently camped in a redwood canyon in Monterey County, and was awed by the natural landscaping of the understory growth in the riparian and redwood plant communities. On steep hillside and in the darkest shade, every inch of ground was covered with redwood sorrel. Sword ferns and flowering plants clustered along the stream banks and at the sun-dappled edge of the forest. Closer examination revealed many ferns and shrubs and a few other trees compatible with redwoods. Why can't we duplicate this fantastic display of nature in our own backyards? The answer is we can, if we are aware of the natural requirements for plant growth under redwoods, and select appropriate species.

Redwood trees grow in cool climates, usually near the coast from Monterey County in California to Southern Oregon where rainfall is high and may be supplemented by summer fog. The trees and understory plants are adapted to our Mediterranean climate of warm, dry summers and mild, wet winters. In the Bay area, redwoods are found in valleys only a few miles inland from the coast, mainly on the south side of Mt. Tamalpais. Nicasio is their northern limit, and they are absent on Point Reyes Peninsula.

In addition to climatic factors, species of plants living under redwoods require shade tolerance and resistance to the resins from decomposed cones and needles. These chemical substances in the soil, called allelopaths, function as inhibitors of seed germination, thereby diminishing competition from their own seedlings and those of other trees and plants.

Soil factors are important for plant growth under redwoods. Prime redwood forests flourish in deep alluvial soil at the bottom of canyons. Partially decomposed twigs and cones continuously pile up creating thick, loose mulch that air and water can easily penetrate. The soil environment supports many kinds of microorganisms including fungi, bacteria and an array of detritus-feeders and decomposers. It is a living soil. You should keep the soil loose with added mulch and protect from compaction.

Here are some choice native understory plants of redwoods. If you don't live in a redwood tree area, these plants may be of interest as understory for trees such as maples, elderberry, hazelnut, alder and bay laurel. Don't try to grow them under oaks and madrone trees that cannot tolerate the amount of water most of these plants need.

Ground Cover Plants

- Redwood Sorrel (*Oxalis oregana*) is my favorite plant because of its thick carpet of foliage spreading from creeping rootstock. The beautiful three-leaflet pattern resembles a shamrock. However, the Irish shamrock is a clover, a member of the pea family totally unrelated to oxalis. There are many weedy species of oxalis that are not welcome in gardens. The leaves are sensitive to light and fold up like little umbrellas when exposed to bright sunlight. They remain open in shade. White to pink flowers appear in March and April.
- Wild Ginger (*Asarum caudatum*) unfortunately has no ginger taste, but the stems and roots have a spicy aroma that may account for its name. The dark green, heart-shaped leaves are very attractive. In early spring, if you look carefully under the leaves, you will find a most surprising flower. It is maroon with long spurs on each of its three pointed lobes, thus commonly called long-tailed ginger.
- Redwood Violet (*Viola sempervirens*)—the name refers to its evergreen growth. The lemon-yellow flowers and rounded

leaves make a cheerful mat under the trees and along the paths in the more open areas of the forest.
- False Lily-of-the-Valley (*Maianthemum dilatatum*) is a wonderful thick ground cover that likes wet soil. In Marin County it grows in some coastal marshes of Point Reyes, but in Mendocino County it is found under the redwoods in partial shade. The name means "May flower ivy."

Other Low-Growing Plants for Shade and Partial Shade

- Inside-Out Flower (*Vancouveria planipetala*)—the small white flowers look like they have been turned inside out. This plant reaches a height of about twelve inches and grows in dense clumps. It is suitable also for rock gardens. Leaves are tiny leaflets resembling maidenhair fern.
- Wake Robin (*Trillium ovatum*) is a member of the lily family with three large leaves below a three-petal white flower that appears in early spring. Deep rooted, it disappears in winter.
- Clintonia (*Clintonia andrewsiana*)—this plant with no common name is an early blooming lily with rose-colored flowers and blue fruits. The China blue porcelain-like berries are very handsome. Strap-like basal leaves die back in winter.
- False Solomon's Seal (*Smilacina stellata* and *S. racemosis*) are fat-leaf and thin-leaf species of handsome, shade loving plants that may be two to three feet tall with white blossoms and red berries. *Smilacina* is a different species from the true Solomon's Seal of the East Coast

Shrubs for Shade and Partial Shade of the Redwoods

- Coffeeberry (*Rhamnus californica*) and Huckleberry (*Vaccinium ovatum*) are especially attractive evergreen shrubs that grow well under trees. Wild Azalea (*Rhododendron occidentalis*) is our native azalea in the redwoods. It is deciduous but has lacy foliage and white to pink flowers in April and May.

CHAPTER TEN

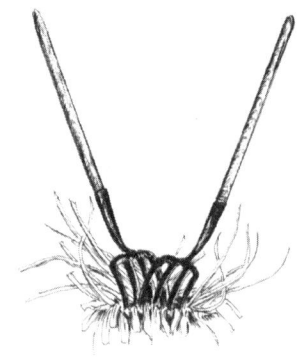

Propagation

Divide and Conquer those Perennials

by Diane Lynch

One of the great pleasures of gardening is sharing bounty from the garden with fellow gardeners and friends. In the Bay area where we have mild winters, fall is the ideal time to divide perennials. They will benefit from the winter rains (assuming we have some) and be rooted in and ready to take off in the spring. For this primer on division we will also include some bulbs, corms and rhizomes, such as iris.

An annual completes its life cycle in one year or growing season. Marigolds are planted from seed in the spring, bloom, make seed and die before winter. A biennial starts its life cycle one year and completes it the next. Hollyhocks are usually biennials: they are planted but do not bloom the first year, and then bloom, set seed and die the following year. Technically, herbaceous perennials are plants that live three or more years, have a fibrous root system and die to the ground in the winter, such as anenome and peonies. But some perennials are evergreen in our climate and some retain a small crown such as shasta daisies, yarrow and penstemon. None of this technical stuff matters much—just get out there and divide those overcrowded plants, saving yourself some money and enriching your garden and others" in the process.

There are several reasons to divide plants:

- blooms are diminishing in size and number
- they have outgrown their space in the garden
- you want more to plant in other places or share

The general rule on dividing is to divide spring bloomers in the fall and fall bloomers in the spring, but those rules can be bent a bit. Because we get no summer rain, it is harder for plants to establish themselves when divided in the spring. Dividing in the fall takes care of that problem and minimizes maintenance of the newly planted divisions. Fall bloomers such as chrysanthemums will need to be divided just after blooming or in early spring. Since our winters are mild, we have little worry about things freezing when divided in the fall. About the worst that can happen if you divide at the wrong time is that you will lose a year of blooms and a few of the divisions.

Water plants to be divided thoroughly the day before dividing and cut back foliage and any flowers. A cool, cloudy or foggy day is perfect to minimize stress.

Look carefully at how the plant grows for clues as to how to divide it. Plants that reproduce by making more of themselves, such as yarrow, shasta daisy, daylily, moraea, lamb's ears, ornamental clump grasses and iris need to be dug up and either cut, teased or pried apart, depending on how big the clump is and how firmly intertwined the roots are. Sometimes you can use two garden forks placed back to back to pry a clump apart. A pruning saw can be used to saw a tough clump (such as moraea or large grasses) apart, or a shovel or hatchet to chop it in half or quarters. If the clump is too large to dig out you can dig up divisions around the base to reduce its overall size. Some plants, such as red hot poker, prefer this treatment.

Pull or cut off any decaying parts and replant or pot your divisions spacing them out to allow for future growth. Be sure to plant at the same depth. It's usually a good idea to cut back top growth by about half so the plant puts its energy into root production.

In the case of iris, divide just after they bloom in the spring. Be sure to plant them just below the surface after removing any rotting areas and cutting into pieces with a single fan of leaves and a couple of "eyes" or buds. Cut two-thirds of the tops off and plant with the top in the direction you want the plant to grow. Bulbs such as daffodils are divided after the green foliage turns yellow in early summer. Bulbs will have little bulblets that can be detached from the main bulb, replanted at the same depth and spaced a few inches apart to allow for growth.

~ *Propagation* ~

Orchids such as cymbidiums are best divided just after they bloom and when they have outgrown their pots. Use a large kitchen knife, cut off any dead bulbs and divide the remainder into clumps with at least three bulbs. Dust cuts with sulfur to discourage rot and pot in a commercial orchid mix of bark and peat moss. Some people believe orchids bloom best when their pots are a little snug so don't leave too much room in the new pots.

Things that are woody or grow from a single stem, such as sage, don't lend themselves to division unless the plant is sending up little plants or suckers around the parent plant. You can dig up some of the little plants and leave the parent alone. If the parent is not good-looking anymore, you can dig it out, leave the babies in place and transplant a few to replace the parent. Some plants, such as butterfly weed (*Asclepsias*) and gas plant (*Dictamnus*) have a deep taproot and do not like to be disturbed; they will take a couple of years to bloom again and are best divided by taking root cuttings.

After dividing be sure to top dress with a nice thick layer of compost or mulch (all except iris which like to be near the surface) and keep well watered.

Save Seeds for the Tastiest Harvest

BY MAGGIE AGRO

If you think the fruit and vegetables you eat today just don't taste as good as those you ate when you were a kid, you're probably right.

Since 1960, the range of crop varieties available to and grown by farmers has steadily decreased. Only three percent of the varieties of fruits and vegetables cultivated for food in 1900 are still around today.

Genetic diversity, the multiple strains or varieties of a food crop, is nature's way of providing that no one individual carries all of the traits of a particular species. This ensures that species will be able to change and adapt to new environments, new pests and changing climates. When our crops become less diverse, they become more susceptible to pests and diseases and our food supply becomes more vulnerable.

Take, for example, the Irish potato famine, caused by a blight, which destroyed the particular strain of potatoes grown in Ireland. By introducing a new strain from Peru, not susceptible to the blight, the food supply was gradually restored and the famine ended.

According to the Food and Agriculture Organization of the United Nations (FAO) the "conservation of genetic diversity is a moral obligation to future generations of people." Since 1983, the FAO has been developing a worldwide system for safeguarding and using plant resources and information sharing.

In New Mexico, Seeds of Change, founded in 1989, is growing plants, collecting and trading seeds with organic growers from around the world. They are saving many plants from extinction and are working to produce new, nutrient rich strains.

Using the same techniques as an organic home gardener, they enrich the soil with compost and use natural mulches to keep in mois-

~ *Propagation* ~

ture; they observe moisture and sun and shade patterns to make the best use of growing conditions. Then they let their plants go to seed and take careful steps to preserve the seed they harvest.

You can help preserve diversity by selecting the best species to grow for your area. Choose heirloom or heritage varieties when possible. Try to reduce the need for purchasing seed by saving seed from all that you grow or buy. By planting the seed that you save, you become a gentle observer of nature's rhythms. You learn to read your plants and their environment.

If you want to start with something easy, try beans or peas. Make it a fun project. Next year when you plant them, you will probably find them a choice spot, give them a little more attention, and get much more satisfaction from growing them. And they will probably taste better. You will find that your level of satisfaction grows with your involvement.

Try saving early-bearing plants to encourage that trait. Mark your seed-saving plants with a ribbon or tie so that they are not accidentally harvested. Keep only the seeds from plants that have done well in your garden and those that are most resistant to insects. Always keep more than you need because it's not unusual to find that only half of most home-saved seeds will grow.

Most seeds will dry adequately if spread on a paper towel for a week. Turn seeds and replace paper if necessary. Large seeds take longer.

You can store seed in baby food jars or margarine tubs but be sure to label all containers with seed name, and year harvested. Seeds stored in paper will absorb moisture from the air and dry out as moisture changes. These changes gradually destroy the viability of the seed.

Remember that seeds from hybrid plants will not produce the same crop next year. Hybrid tomato seed, for example, may produce something tough or tasteless. If you avoid hybrids, you will be able to grow the same tomato year after year, even if different varieties were planted close together.

Go Forth and Propagate

~

BY LEE OLIPHANT AND DIANE LYNCH

Propagation is one of the most fascinating and mysterious facets of gardening. It is the process of creating new plants in order to share them with friends and neighbors and to enrich your own garden. The two basic ways to propagate plants are sexual (seeds), and asexual, using leaves, stems or roots to generate a new plant.

There are advantages to propagating through cuttings. It is faster than planting from seeds and newly created plants from cuttings will be perfect clones of the parent plant. Plants can be started from cuttings because the tissue contains growth-regulating hormones that are stimulated to become root cells. With a little effort and practice, you can create a garden that is lavish and abundant.

General Guidelines for Cutting Propagation

Use healthy plants as your source. Watering the plant thoroughly the day before taking cuttings will improve your chances of successful rooting. Take cuttings on a cloudy day if possible and keep them shaded until ready to prepare. Use a light potting soil containing peat moss and vermiculite or mix your own, using equal parts of builders' sand, peat moss and vermiculite in pots with open drain holes. Lateral or side shoots tend to root better than terminal shoots. After planting the cuttings, the soil must be kept moist for proper rooting.

You don't need a greenhouse to propagate new plants from cuttings. A plastic bag can be used to make a mini-greenhouse to keep the humidity suitably high. Since a plant cannot take up water until its root system is formed, a moist environment is essential. The plastic should not touch the leaves and can be closed with a rubber band. Open the bag for an hour each day to supply air and prevent fungus.

~ *Propagation* ~

Propagation of Softwood and Semi-hardwood Cuttings

Softwood cuttings can be rooted from spring to late summer. They are the soft, flexible, new growth taken during the growing season. Plants that can be propagated with softwood cuttings are cytisus, erica, forsythia, hydrangea, geranium, lantana, lavatera, and viburnum.

Early autumn through the early fall is the best time to take semi-hardwood cuttings. Semi-hardwood means firm enough to snap if bent sharply. If the stem bends too much, it is too mature for rooting. Plants that root easily from softwood cuttings include: currant, grape, mulberry, rose, lavender, barberry, cherry, and fuchsia.

Using a sharp knife, cut healthy stems from two to six inches long. Make the cut about one-quarter inch below a leaf. Remove all but two or three leaves and any flowers. If the plant is oozing fluid, set it aside for an hour to dry the wound. Use of rooting hormone, available in powder form in any nursery, may increase chances of successful rooting. Put a small amount of rooting hormone in a saucer or small plastic bag for dipping, to avoid contamination of the container. Be certain that the powder touches the nodes (growing points) where the leaves were removed. Tap off excess. Too much rooting hormone may actually inhibit rooting. Use a pencil to make a hole in the damp soil of small individual pots or larger six inch pots, and insert the cutting(s). Up to six cuttings can be put into each large pot. Gently press the soil around the cutting. Keep the soil moist, not soaked. Once the cuttings have rooted, harden them off by placing them in the sun for a few hours each day. Carefully separate before planting.

Propagation of Hardwood Cuttings

Many deciduous trees and shrubs may be propagated from hardwood (dormant) cuttings. Plants that root easily from hardwoods are: willows, fig, dracaena, mulberry, sycamore, and poplar.

Select cuttings for rooting just after leaves fall. Cut them off just above a bud at the junction between the current and the previous season's growth. Remove the top inch or two of each stem and cut the stems into six inch to nine inch lengths with two or three nodes. Dip the bottom end in rooting hormone. You can bundle the stems together and store them upright in a pot filled with sand in a cool, dry place. In early spring the cuttings may be planted in a well-drained trench outside, about six to nine inches apart. Leave the top bud of each cutting exposed. Keep soil moist until stems are ready for transplanting to their permanent home.

Propagation Through Layering

From autumn to spring, vines, berries, and currants can be propagated successfully through layering. Layering occurs naturally in some plants and has the advantage of allowing rooting of new plant while still attached to the mother plant. Plants that lend themselves to layering as a means of propagation are rhododendron, honeysuckle, wisteria, grape, heart-leaf philodendron and clematis.

Take a pliant branch and gently bend it until it touches the earth, leaving the last six to twelve inches of branch above ground. Dig a shallow trench for the branch. Remove the lower leaves from the part of the branch that will be covered with soil. Nick the stem and apply rooting hormone to the wound. Peg it into the hole with bent wire and stake the stem's tip vertically. Secure it with a tie. Cover with a little loosened, amended soil and keep moist. When the plant has developed roots, the branch can be cut away from the original plant below the soil and moved to another location.

Propagation Through Leaf Cuttings

Many indoor plants and succulents can be propagated from a single leaf cutting. A rex begonia, sansevierias, jade plant, wandering Jew, African violet, peperomia and crassulas or coleus can all be propagated using this method. Dust the stem end of the leaf in rooting hormone. Place the stem section of the leaf into potting soil vertically. Keep the leaf moist and out of direct sunlight for several weeks until the leaf has rooted or new shoots appear.

By experimenting with various methods of plant propagation, you will delight in enriching your garden and sharing its abundance.

CHAPTER ELEVEN

Weeds and Invasives

Exotic Invasives and Misplaced Plants

BY DIANE LYNCH

There are few topics that stir up stronger passions among gardeners than invasive plants or weeds. No gardener is exempt from the aggravation of attempting to control unwanted plants in the garden. There is really no such thing as a maintenance-free garden as all gardens require at least periodic weeding. California's wild lands are under attack from exotic invaders, which lack the natural controls that might exist in their native habitats, and threaten ecosystems by forcing out natives. Probably the most visible of these invaders is the ubiquitous eucalyptus that has planted itself into enormous stands all over the Bay area. These Australian natives have altered ecosystems by shedding highly flammable bark, slurping up water, thus depleting water tables, and chemically suppressing desirable plants. Millions of dollars a year are spent removing this plant from our parklands.

Sometimes a weed is called a misplaced plant. *Weeds of the West* defines a weed as "a plant that interferes with management objectives for a given area of land at a given point in time." The difference between a weed and an invasive is a matter of degree, since all weeds are invading an area where they are not wanted. The real problem occurs when a plant happens to find conditions that are ideal and the local, desirable, native plants cannot out-compete the weed and keep it under control. Both the California Department of Food and Agriculture and the U. S. government keep lists of "noxious weeds," which are defined as troublesome, aggressive, intrusive, detrimental or destructive to agriculture, silviculture (trees), or important native species. The California list contains over one hundred and forty species considered to be detrimental. Interestingly, some plants listed are natives such as the native iris, *Iris douglasiana*. Location is an

~ *Weeds and Invasives* ~

important factor, as some plants will multiply out of control in some areas and not others, depending on growing conditions. For example, pampas grass and its close relative jubata grass are a real problem in coastal areas of California but inland areas of the state don't have a problem, with the exception of the American River near Sacramento.

The most visible invasive weeds in the Bay area are eucalyptus, pampas grass and jubata grass, broom (primarily French, but also Scotch and Spanish) and Himalayan blackberry. Pampas grass was introduced to California by the horticultural trade and the plumes were used to decorate Victorian parlors. It grows into large clumps that have razor sharp edges and the tiny windborne seeds blow by the millions to start new plants all over the place. Broom was introduced as a landscaping plant in the nineteenth century and has escaped to open space where a seedling can grow to an inch in diameter and five feet or more in a year's time. Easy to pull when young, the biggest problem is its prolific seed dispersal coupled with rapid growth. Broom removal is a popular volunteer pastime in our parklands and many Boy Scouts have earned their Eagle badges removing broom. Broom is quick to take over disturbed land along roadsides and creates a fire hazard where it has forced out native shrubbery. The Himalayan blackberry grows rampantly into enormous thickets covering whatever is in its path. While it does supply food for birds and is certainly tasty to people, it also provides perfect habitat for rats: food, water, shelter all together. Since many animals feed on blackberries, they also disseminate the seeds widely.

Another exotic invasive that is a problem in the Bay area is yellow starthistle, which is a nasty, spiny weed to encounter while walking and can cause a fatal nervous disorder in horses. Gorse, which resembles a spiny broom and ruins pasturelands, is also a problem along the coast where its seeds are ejected in large quantity and it can remain viable for thirty years. Japanese honeysuckle, readily available at nurseries, is one of the worst invaders, and the red passionflower is becoming a problem. Acacia, sometimes recommended for erosion control, is very invasive and sends up starts along its root system. Even pittosporum is showing up in oak groves.

According to the Marin County Stormwater Pollution Prevention Program (MCSTOPPP), a lot of commonly used plants can be invasive, especially when planted near water sources such as streams and springs. Periwinkle, the common groundcover with purple flowers, can be invasive along streams and is frequently seen in such locations. Other groundcovers, which can escape and smother other plants, including desirable natives, include ice plant, trailing gazania, silver spreader, African daisy, German, Algerian and English ivies. Groundcovers can have the additional disadvantage of providing shelter and sometimes food for rats.

Some perennials to think twice about planting include bamboo (particularly the running varieties; ask for clumping varieties which spread much slower), Mexican evening primrose, some mints, pampas grass, of course, as well as fountain grass. Shrubs and trees to avoid include oleander, all varieties of broom (amazingly, some local nurseries carry broom), rockspray, cotoneaster, myoporum, acacia, black locust, eucalyptus, tree tobacco, tree of heaven, salt cedar and tamarisk. Some of these plants may be fine in controlled situations away from open spaces and streams, but all can naturalize and spread rampantly under favorable conditions.

The two most important things you can do to keep weeds under control, after proper plant selection, are mulching and deadheading. A thick layer, four to six inches, of organic matter will make it easy to pull unwanted plants. Deadheading spent flowers will prevent them from seeding all over the place. Some plants, such as Japanese anemone and many grasses, produce fine seeds that can blow some distance and become a problem in areas outside your own garden. Another factor in the spread of unwanted species is the disturbance of the soil. When soil is plowed or turned, weed seeds are moved to the surface so they germinate readily.

A Place for Invasives?

by Barbara J. Euser

Is there ever a time to plant invasives—plants that are known to spread—in the garden? I believe the answer is a qualified "yes."

There is never a time to plant exotic, that is non-native, invasives. Exotic invasives such as pampas grass and French and Scottish broom were sold by local nurseries in the past, before their destructive nature was understood. Plants like these are so hardy they replace California natives in open spaces. Today, for example, volunteers spend hundreds of hours pulling out broom growing on Mt. Tamalpais in an effort to recreate an environment conducive to California native plants. There is no place for exotic invasives in California and they should be pulled out or dug up and destroyed.

Native invasive plants are another story: there are situations in which they can be both practical and desirable. In my garden, I have a lot of space to fill. As I select plants for inclusion, I look for California natives and Mediterranean species that will reproduce or expand naturally in our Bay area climate. It is the rate at which some plants reproduce that qualifies them as invasives: they will invade the empty spaces of my garden over time. Some send out roots that can sprout leaves, others reproduce by rhizomes, some produce easily germinating seeds, some send out runners. Planting invasives is a calculated risk. I have learned that the invasion of my garden is a slow march at best.

California Natives

Woodland strawberry: This year I had all the ivy removed from my garden. Like mint, each node on each shoot of ivy is capable of growing its own roots and sprouting leaves if it is in contact with the soil. So even though the ivy has been removed once, I will have to be vigilant in pulling up any new shoots I see. I searched for a native plant that could successfully compete against ivy. The apparently delicate *Fragaria californica*, or woodland strawberry, is reputed to be tough enough. Once it establishes itself as a mat of interlocking runners of adjacent plants, it should keep the ivy out. So far, the half dozen I planted have produced tiny new plants that are rooting and extending additional runners out about three feet in diameter around each plant.

Redwood sorrel: The trait which makes the exotic *Oxalis pexcaprae* (formerly *O. cernua)*, Bermuda buttercup, a troublesome weed, makes its native cousin *Oxalis oregana*, redwood sorrel, desirable in my garden. When we ripped out the ivy underneath our redwood tree, again I searched for something tough. Redwood sorrel, as the name suggests, is a native of coastal forests from Washington to California, and a logical choice for this spot. It is a larger plant, with broader leaves and showier white or pink flowers than its weedy relative. The time I spend pulling *Oxalis cernua* out of my garden made me pause when I considered planting *Oxalis oregana* under the redwood. Although redwood sorrel is not as prolific in putting out roots that will sprout into new plants as its relative, I am very pleased with my choice.

California fuchsia: Another invasive which I have planted is the California native *Epilobium canum* (formerly *Zauschneria californica*), also known as California fuchsia. Its dusty gray foliage has a wild and rangy look about it. However, the brilliant scarlet trumpet-shaped flowers are a great favorite of hummingbirds. I planted these fuchsias for the birds' enjoyment. Two seasons after I planted them, I noticed numerous gray wisps of plants emerging in the general vicinity of the older plants. A few of these I allowed to stay and maybe they will succeed. But others I pulled up as weeds. That certainly is one way to deal with any invasives. Or, if you find you suffer an embarrassment of riches in terms of free new plants, you can always dig them up and give them away.

~ Weeds and Invasives ~

Mediterranean Species

Valerian: I planted valerian, *Centhranthus ruber*, because I admire its plentiful pink spikes of blossoms in springtime. I have seen it proliferating in road cuts and on steep dry banks. I like it because it is an herb with medicinal properties, primarily known for its calming, sleep inducing effects. Despite its reputation as an invasive, only a few new young plants have sprouted around the bases of the four I originally planted. I look forward to a large block of plants developing.

Erigeron: Although it is commonly called Santa Barbara daisy, *Erigeron karvinskianus* is a native of Mexico. Considered an invasive plant, I have found it more prolific in self-seeding than the valerian. Often it appears that a single plant is increasing its diameter, but when I lift up the edges of the plant I discover that new plants have sprouted under the cover of the mother plant, producing, in effect, a colony. To my delight, the mounds of small pink and white blossoms are expanding.

Mint: Spearmint, *Mentha spicata*, in my garden, as well as many other species of mint, is aggressively invasive. I find myself pulling mint out of the area in which it serves as a ground cover, treating it as a weed when it moves to spots where I am encouraging other plants. On other occasions, I clip it to flavor tea or use in a salad or savory dish. In every case, I appreciate its fragrance and its glossy green foliage and I'm happy to have it in abundant supply.

CHAPTER TWELVE

Insects, Pests and Their Control

Honey Bees and Their Kin

~

BY VIRGINIA HAVEL

As I sat in our patio last week, I could not ignore the persistent humming of fuzzy black and yellow bumblebees flitting from blossom to blossom in a dwarf lime tree. The potted tree was in dense fragrant flower, and the bumblebees seemed delighted to have discovered such a rich source of nectar. How differently I responded to these friendly bees compared to their nasty wasp cousins, the yellow jackets, that try to steal every bite of our outdoor meal and threaten us with their venomous stings.

Both bees and wasps belong to the insect order, Hymenoptera. There are more than one hundred thousand species of Hymenoptera, and it includes many kinds of bees as well as wasps, hornets, ants, and others, with a variety of behaviors, life styles (solitary and social), and ecological roles (plant and nectar feeders, scavengers, carnivores and parasites).

Hymenoptera means membranous wings. There are two forewings and two hind wings. Bees and wasps belong to a subgroup of Hymenoptera characterized by the possession of a constriction or "wasp waist" between the thorax and the second segment of the abdomen. Bees originated during the Cretaceous period when mammals and flowering plants were first appearing. They evolved from one group of wasps that lost its predatory habits of preying on or parasitizing other insects as food for their larvae, in favor of feeding their larvae nectar and pollen.

Bees actually co-evolved with flowers, each becoming dependent on the other. Specialized structures on the legs and abdomen allowed the bees to gather and transport pollen to their nests. Mouth parts for sipping nectar and for chewing are other bee characteristics. Many species of flowers evolved glands for producing fragrant nectar; colorful stripes or dot patterns on their petals act as nectar guides for bees to follow into the flower, and at the same time pick up pollen. When pollen is carried to other flowers of the same species, fertilization occurs. Pollination may be effected by other insects, birds and wind, but bees are the most important instrument for reproduction in the plant world, and they play a major role in agriculture.

Honeybees have the most highly organized social structure of all bee species. About fifty thousand individuals live in one hive made up of mostly sterile females, some drones (males) and one queen, in addition to the immature stages (egg, larva, pupa). The sole job of the queen is to mate and lay eggs. She produces tens of thousands in her lifespan. The stingless drone's only function is to mate with a new queen when one is needed. Once a queen is fertilized during a nuptial flight, drones have no further function and indeed are killed off by workers every winter. The main activities of a hive are carried out by thousands of female worker bees. They do all food gathering, protect the hive from intruders, construct the nest and wax honeycombs, produce the honey, and feed the larval bees and queen. Worker bees are certainly the hardest worked creatures of the natural world. They live only about six weeks before they wear out! It has been estimated that to make one pound of honey, a bee would have to fly the equivalent distance of twice around the world.

One of the most remarkable functions of workers is to raise the kinds of bees needed for a colony. They do this by selecting the diet larval bees receive, thus giving credence to the saying, "You are what you eat." Worker larvae receive a standard diet of protein-rich food called "royal jelly" for three days and then a mixture of honey and pollen called "bee-bread". After pupating, they emerge from their wax cell in twenty-one days. Drone candidates are reared from unfertilized eggs. Their diet is the same as workers, but they emerge in twenty-four days, somewhat larger than workers.

If the queen dies, several new queens are produced. To make new queens, larger wax cells are constructed, and selected larvae placed in them to be fed only on royal jelly. This seems to increase the size of

~ Insects, Pests and Their Control ~

the bee and speed up development. The fertile queens emerge from the pupa stage in only sixteen days. The first task of a new queen is to establish dominance over her sister queens. Only one can become queen of the hive. The others are either killed by the successful ruler or fly off with some of the workers in the colony to establish a new nest. Before settling down at a new location, the departing queen and her workers form a tight ball of bees called a swarm. The swarm roosts in trees or other locations for a few days while scouts explore for a nesting site. Bee swarms can be captured by beekeepers at this stage.

In the last forty years, wild bee populations have declined to about five percent of their former numbers due to misuse of pesticides, loss of habitat, predation and disease. It is important to preserve bees because cross-pollination increases crop yields, enhances reproduction in most flowering plants, and increases biodiversity in gene pools. By limiting the use of pesticides and by planting a variety of fragrant, brightly colored flowers in your garden, you can help the recovery of bee populations.

Little Miss Muffett and Friends

by Jan Specht

We all have our own reactions to spiders, ranging from fascination to fright. But regardless of whether you're attracted to them or repelled by them, spiders perform a very useful pest control service, both indoors and out.

Spiders in the garden are beneficial organisms. They eat only live insects, mites and sometimes each other, but not plants. Potential garden pests make up the largest portion of their diet, so by avoiding pesticides you can increase the presence of all beneficial organisms in the garden. Most spiders prefer dark, shady locations. Natural enemies of spiders are certain insects, birds, reptiles, scorpions and some vertebrates. There are over three thousand species of spiders in North America alone and an estimated one hundred and seventy thousand species worldwide. No wonder we see them everywhere!

Hunting spiders (as opposed to web spinning spiders), such as wolf spiders and jumping spiders, physically attack their prey rather than trapping it in a web. The wolf spider may be seen waiting in the sun, then chasing down its prey. The daddy longlegs, which is not a spider, hunts small insects also. Spiders are often more prevalent after the first few rains in the fall. Burrow-living spiders may wander for a time during winter if they had to abandon a wet burrow.

Spiders indoors are more of a nuisance than dangerous. Control measures are possible that do not require pesticides. Indeed, chemical control is so temporary that it is impractical, costly and possibly dangerous. Mechanical controls are more effective and safer. Inspect doors and windows for a snug fit and use weather-stripping if necessary. Be sure screens do not have holes. Check entry sites for water pipes, electrical and phone lines and caulk around these areas. Caulk

~ *Insects, Pests and Their Control* ~

other cracks and small openings. These measures will decrease spider entry as well as the insects that spiders need for food. It is also helpful to keep woodpiles away from the house and inspect firewood before bringing it indoors. Keep the area next to your house foundation free of heavy vegetation and debris (including leaf and other garden litter). Outdoor lighting attracts insects, which attract spiders. When possible, keep lighting fixtures off the house and away from windows and doorways or try a yellow bulb.

In spite of these measures, you will still have some spiders indoors. Some people gently trap spiders in a jar, then slip a piece of paper over the mouth of the jar and release the spider outdoors. For the arachnophobics among us, it is possible to keep the spider count indoors down by avoiding chemical sprays and using environmentally friendly means. The easiest way is to vacuum the spider and the web. The dust inside the vacuum bag will kill the spider by suffocating it. Spiders are most likely to be found in areas that are left undisturbed for relatively long periods of time, such as behind and under furniture, in corners, and in storage areas or boxes. Vacuuming these areas more often will help. Remember that spiders are indoors because there is a food source there for them. Tasty treats are cupboard pests like silverfish, clothes moths, and even fruit flies. If you keep ripening fruit on the kitchen counter, try storing it in a sealed paper bag.

All spiders produce venom but few are harmful because their fangs are too short to pierce human skin. The most harmful one in California is the female black widow spider. The body, excluding the legs, is approximately one-half inch long. The male is smaller than the female, has different coloring, does have venom but its fangs are too small to bite humans. All immature and adult black widows have the hourglass mark on the underside of the abdomen. The poisonous adult female has a red or orange hourglass and all the others are yellow to yellow orange. Black widows generally are very timid and bite only when touched, usually accidentally. They live in dark, dry, sheltered places. Always wear gloves and a long-sleeved shirt when working in such areas as the garage, woodpiles, around rocks, crawl spaces and meter boxes. Also, shake out gloves and outdoor shoes before putting them on if they are stored in the garage. If bitten, seek medical help. Most people do not develop severe symptoms. Some pain, redness and swelling at the bite site may go no further. However, pain that spreads from the bite site to other parts of the body along with muscle spasms indicate a more serious bite. Other symptoms such as elevated blood pressure, fever, shortness of breath, and restlessness may occur.

The name brown recluse spider is familiar to most people even though there have been no confirmed bites from this spider in California. Confirmation requires catching the spider in the act and capturing it for identification. There are no known populations of brown recluse spiders in California, even though entomologists have searched for them.

The yellow sac spider is a common indoor spider found worldwide. It is nocturnal and can be seen running on walls or ceilings at night and drops to the floor if disturbed. Bites occur at night if the spider encounters a sleeping human. The bite causes a small area of redness, swelling and itching. Sometimes pain or a small blister occurs which may cause a small ulcer. These bites heal over several days to a few weeks and are not serious.

Tarantulas in California can inflict bites but they are not likely to be serious. Greater distress is caused when an annoyed tarantula rubs its legs against the hairs on its abdomen, sending small airborne barbs into the victim's eyes or nose.

The poor spider often is blamed for a skin lesion even though there are numerous insects, other arthropods and medical disorders that could be the cause. Not all bites are noted at the time they occur, but if a spider is caught in the act, try to capture it for identification. Even a crushed spider inside clothing may be identifiable. Sometimes it is more important to know what it isn't (brown recluse) rather than what it is.

Scale Insects in the Garden

by Jan Specht

There are two groups of scales commonly found in our gardens—armored and soft—and there are many different species of scales in each group. Each can be a serious pest on all types of woody plants and shrubs. Because these insects look so different from other insects, many people do not recognize them.

Adult female armored scales are less than one-eighth inch in diameter and have a hard round cover that can usually be removed from the body. This hard cover provides some protection from pesticides and predators. Armored scales hatch from eggs, crawl a short distance, then lose their legs and form the hard cover; once in place, they are immobile. They produce several generations a year.

Adult female soft scales have a smooth or cottony soft surface and are one-quarter inch or less in diameter. They are more convex than armored scales and lack the hard cover. The soft types retain their barely visible legs and can move a little, usually from foliage to bark before leaves drop in the fall. They usually produce only one generation a year. Soft scales, but not armored, produce large amounts of honeydew. Adult male scales are tiny with one pair of wings and a long tail filament. They do not feed and live only a few hours.

Scales cause damage because their piercing mouthparts suck fluid from the plant and some inject toxic saliva into the plant. A heavy infestation of armored scales will cause leaves to yellow and drop, and may cause tree twigs and limbs to die, and bark to crack and produce a gummy substance. Many armored scales also attack fruits, leaving blemishes and halos, which don't really damage the fruit, but are aesthetically unpleasing. Small numbers of scales often cause no damage but large numbers of some armored scales can kill plants. Soft scales reduce tree vigor by infesting leaves and twigs but rarely kill the tree. However, they produce large amounts of honeydew which drips onto leaves, fruits and branches, as well as cars or sidewalks that are under the tree. Honeydew supports the growth of black sooty mold, a fungus that makes the leaves look dirty, and it attracts ants, which chase natural predators away.

To minimize scales in the garden, grow a wide variety of flowering plants near scale-infested plants. Begin with spring blooming plants to invite beneficial insects into your garden early. Adult parasitic wasps live longer and lay more eggs when they have plant nectar to feed upon. Avoid over fertilizing because scales reproduce more quickly on plants with high nitrogen levels in the leaves and buds. Fertilize with compost or a slow-release fertilizer. Dust control is crucial for natural enemies, so wash plants if foliage is dusty. Avoid using pesticides because they kill the natural enemies as well as pest insects.

There are several natural predators of scales. One is a tiny, shiny black lady beetle with red, orange or yellow spots on the back. Another type of lady beetle has a reddish head and underside with a grayish back densely covered with tiny hairs. The "twice stabbed" lady beetle is shiny black with two red spots on the back and reddish underneath. The larvae of certain lady beetles can be found under the female soft scales feeding on the scale eggs and crawlers. Many parasitic wasps are also natural enemies of scales. You will know they are present if you see round exit holes in the armored covers. The emerging wasp makes the hole; if you flip the armored cover over, you will see the immature wasp.

It is important to check your woody plants during dormancy. Scales are easy to see when deciduous plants have lost their leaves. Citrus, avocado and other plants that do not have winter dormancy can be monitored anytime by examining the entire plant, including the fruit. Monitor for ants during the growing season. The numbers of some kinds of scales can increase dramatically within a few months when ants protect scales. Controlling ants is usually enough to control the soft scales because natural enemies then can take over. Wrap the tree or shrub trunk with fabric tree wrap or duct tape, then apply

~ *Insects, Pests and Their Control* ~

Tanglefoot or Stick'em to the wrap. Keep leaves and debris off the sticky substance to avoid ants using the debris as a bridge. Likewise, prune branches that provide ants a bridge to buildings or the ground.

Small numbers of scale can be rubbed off by hand or with a cotton swab dipped in alcohol. Prune out areas of severe infestation if possible. Insecticidal soap is a least toxic, extremely safe chemical to use and is registered for scale control. Other more toxic pesticides are also registered for use against scales, but they cause more damage to beneficial insects and our environment because the pesticide residue persists. If your scale infestation is extensive, you probably need to use narrow range horticultural oil, a highly refined oil which is a least toxic and very effective treatment. Do not use dormant oils because they are more likely to injure plants. Narrow range oil is effective against most scales, but not against oystershell or olive scales. It is best to spray during dormancy because the adult scales are easier to see and less volume of spray is needed at that time. Sycamore and oak pit scales must be sprayed only during late dormancy, which is after buds swell but before they open. Oil treatments for citrus or avocado trees are applied in spring or summer because these plants do not have a dormant period. For other adult scales, any time during dormancy is good but an ideal time is right after a period of rain or foggy weather. Avoid applying during or just before hot (90°F) or freezing weather. Do not apply to deciduous trees within thirty days before or after using sulfur or certain other fungicides to avoid plant damage.

Oil treatment for the crawler stage on deciduous plants can be applied in spring or summer. However, treatment in these seasons requires more spray volume because foliage is present and timing is critical to kill the susceptible crawlers. Identifying when the crawlers are hatching requires use of double-sided, transparent, sticky tape traps applied tightly around several twigs or branches. The tapes must be changed weekly and examined with a hand lens to identify the crawlers that appear as tiny yellow or orange dots. Spray when a sharp increase in numbers is seen or right after numbers have increased and then begin to decrease.

Spider Mites

~

BY JAN SPECHT

Spider mites are not classified as insects but belong to the arachnid group that includes spiders and ticks. Mites are very common pests in the garden and feed on many different types of plants such as fruit trees, vines, berries, vegetables and ornamental plants.

They are tiny pests and appear as moving dots to the naked eye. With a 10x hand lens they easily can be identified because adults have four sets of legs (insects have three sets), an oval body and two red eyespots near the head end. Females usually have a dark blotch on each side of the body and numerous bristles covering the legs and body. Spider mites are also known as webspinning mites because most species produce a silky web. They live in colonies primarily on the under surface of leaves and a single colony may contain hundreds of them. Eggs appear as tiny translucent spherical drops.

In most of California, spider mites feed and reproduce year round on evergreen plants. In colder areas, the webspinners overwinter as red or orange mated females or as eggs under rough bark and in ground litter. They begin feeding and laying eggs when warm weather returns in spring. They reproduce rapidly in hot weather and usually become numerous June through September. In favorable conditions, a generation takes only a few days.

Spider mites suck nutrient fluid out of leaves. Initial damage is seen as tiny light dots on the affected leaves. As they continue to suck out plant fluids, the leaves turn yellow, dry, and fall off. Leaves, twigs and fruit can be covered with large amounts of webbing. If the plant is water-stressed, the damage is usually worse.

Because mites are so tiny, stippling of the leaves will probably be noticed before the mites are seen. If growing highly susceptible plants (e.g., most fuchsias), it is good to regularly monitor for mites by checking the under surface of a few leaves for webbing. This will allow earlier detection. Use a 10x hand lens to identify them. They may be easier to see if the leaf is shaken so they fall onto a white sheet of paper. When disturbed, they move rapidly.

There are several things one can do to create unfavorable garden conditions for spider mites. Dusty conditions favor mite outbreaks so mulching or using ground covers will decrease dust and provide numerous other benefits. Water appropriately to avoid water-stressed plants. Also, one or two mid-season overhead waterings (early in the day) can decrease dust on foliage. Clean up garden debris so the adult females will have fewer places to over winter. Inspect new plants carefully before adding them to the garden.

Create favorable garden conditions for natural predators of spider mites by avoiding pesticide sprays. These sprays not only kill beneficial organisms, but some (carbaryl, certain organophosphates and some pyrethroids) actually contribute to a favorable environment for the mites leading to dramatic outbreaks within a few days of use. The outbreaks are greatest when the pesticides are applied during hot weather. Spider mites have many natural enemies. Predatory mites attack pest mites but sometimes can be confused with them. The predatory mites have longer legs, pear-shaped bodies and are shiny because they have fewer tiny hairs. They also move faster than the pests. Predaceous mite eggs are pearl colored and oblong. Many predaceous mites also feed on other pests such as the immature forms of scales, thrips and whiteflies. Other important beneficial insects that attack pest mites include six-spotted thrips, larvae and adults of the spider mite destroyer lady beetle, the larvae of certain flies and general predators such as minute pirate bugs, big-eyed bugs and lacewing larvae.

Least toxic treatments for spider mites include insecticidal soap or insecticidal oil. Sulfur dust or spray can be used on some vegetables but will burn curcurbits. These should not be used on plants that are water stressed nor when temperatures exceed 90°F and sulfur should not be used if an oil spray has been applied within thirty days.

Snails, Slugs and Slime

by Jan Specht

Snails and slugs are members of the mollusk group and are similar except slugs lack the external shell. They move by gliding along on a mucous-secreting muscle. The dried mucous becomes a silvery slime trail that tells you they have been dining in your garden. The common brown garden snail (*Helix aspera*) was brought to California as a culinary source from France in the 1850s. Moisture is critical to their survival and is why they are active only at night or during cloudy days. On sunny days they are hiding in moist, shady places. During hot, dry weather they seal themselves off with a membrane while attached to tree trunks, fences or walls. During cold weather, they hibernate in the topsoil. They are among the first pests to begin feeding in spring and the last to stop eating your plants in fall.

The adult snail and slug each lay a mass of about eighty to one hundred eggs and they may do this up to six times a year. The eggs resemble small pearls (about one-eighth inch); they can be seen about one inch below the soil level or under rocks, boards or plant debris and they hatch when they come in contact with moisture. It takes about two years for snails to mature but slugs mature in one year. The garden snail may live as long as twelve years but slugs only live about two years. Given all this, it is easy to see why there are huge numbers of these pests in the garden. Eliminating as many as possible requires persistence.

Snails and slugs damage plants by chewing irregular holes with smooth edges in leaves. They also chew young plant bark, seedlings and fruits that are close to the ground such as strawberries and tomatoes. Citrus trees are especially susceptible.

There are several nontoxic ways to get rid of these pests. The first step is prevention. Eliminate, as much as possible, their daytime hiding

~ *Insects, Pests and Their Control* ~

places such as boards, stones, debris, weedy areas around tree trunks, leafy branches touching the ground and dense ground covers like ivy. They also hide in clumps of nasturtiums, agapanthus, lilies, daffodils and iris. Consider drip irrigation to reduce humidity and moist surfaces they love. Shady areas that you cannot eliminate, such as water meter boxes and the underside of wood decks, also should be checked.

Handpicking at night is a very effective control measure. Water the infested area in the late afternoon and start picking them after ten or eleven at night. You won't find as many if you hunt them earlier. All it takes is a flashlight and gloves or tongs. Dispose of them in a plastic bag in the trash. Alternatively, put them in a bucket of soapy water (they survive plain water) and when they are dead, dispose of them in the compost pile. Large piles of crushed snails and slugs left in the garden will breed flies, but if buried three to four inches in the garden will add nutrients to the soil and avoid flies. Handpicking should be done nightly until the numbers significantly decline (roughly a week); then weekly picking may be enough.

Copper strips are very effective barriers because snails and slugs get an unpleasant reaction if they try to cross them. It is thought that the copper reacts with the mucous causing a flow of electricity. The strips can be used around tree trunks, around the edge of a flowerbed and around the edges of containers. Be sure to handpick the pests from these areas for a few nights before applying the strips. Otherwise you will make them very happy because they are trapped between the strip and the plant. Another barrier method is horticultural fabric for vegetable rows. It allows light and water in but keeps snails and slugs out. Cover seedlings with small cages of old milk cartons, plastic or old window screens.

Whichever barrier you choose, be sure to push it deeply enough into the soil so they cannot burrow under it. Finely crushed eggshells applied around the perimeter of the garden or around each plant work very well and last through spring, summer and fall if your garden has drip irrigation (regular irrigation will wash eggshells away). Barriers of dry ashes or diatomaceous earth can work until they get damp and lose their effectiveness; they are also easily blown by the wind and are hazardous if inhaled.

Snail and slug traps are easy to use. A wooden board or an upside-down flowerpot with one edge on the ground and the other edge slightly raised will attract the pests that can then be scraped into a plastic bag. Beer-baited traps are used to drown snails and slugs. However, they attract these pests within an area of only a few feet and must be refilled regularly to keep the level high enough. If using beer, it is more effective fresh than flat.

There are several baits available. Iron phosphate (Sluggo or Escar-Go) is an effective bait and safe to use around pets and wildlife. This bait causes the pests to stop feeding and they die within a few days. Iron phosphate can be scattered on lawns or on soil around vegetables, fruit trees or ornamentals that need protection. It remains effective for about two weeks, even after irrigation. Avoid baits containing methiocarb because they kill earthworms and beneficial insects. Methiocarb and metaldehyde baits can be hazardous and should not be used if children or pets are around. Avoid getting metaldehyde on plants, especially vegetables. These baits are less effective during hot, dry or cold seasons. If used, these baits should be applied in narrow strips in moist, protected areas or scattered in areas that snails and slugs cross between the sheltered areas and the garden. Regular use of these two chemicals will result in snails and slugs that are resistant to them.

Natural enemies of snails and slugs include ground beetles, snakes, toads, turtles and birds. The ground beetles are one to two inches, black and found in the same moist areas as the snails and slugs. Avoid killing these natural predators.

Any one of the above controls will significantly reduce the snail and slug damage in your garden. The goal should be to reduce their numbers to the point that you see much less damage. It is not possible to completely rid the garden of these pests even by using strong pesticides. Using the above methods will not only control the pests but will protect humans, pets and the environment from toxic chemicals.

Ant Control Without Chemicals

by Jan Specht

Ants are easy to control without the use of toxic pesticides that can harm us and the environment. Control measures differ depending on whether the ants are causing a problem in the garden or in the house.

The Argentine ant is the most common of the two hundred species of ants that occur in California and is the one we all know. These ants differ from other California ants because they have multiple queens in a nest, they move their nests if disturbed, and in winter, several colonies will nest together. When ants leave the nest in large numbers to mate and start new colonies, they have wings and are often mistaken for winged termites. They can be easily distinguished. Ants have elbowed antennae, wings with few veins and smaller hind wings, and a very narrow abdomen.

In the garden, ants protect insect pests that produce honeydew such as aphids, soft scales, whiteflies, and mealy bugs. When ants are present in these infestations, they allow the pests to proliferate and cause more damage; they actually chase away beneficial insects such as lady beetles. If ants are not present and you see only a few insect pests, and if you do not use pesticides in your garden, you can monitor the area for damage and wait until the beneficial insects arrive.

If ants are present, you must eliminate the ants before you can control the other insect pests. Apply a collar around the base of the plant using double-sided sticky tape for a small plant or fabric tree wrap or duct tape for a tree trunk. Then coat the collar with a very sticky substance like Tanglefoot or Stickem. Do not apply these products directly to the plant. Check the sticky material regularly to remove leaves or other debris that the ants could use to cross the barrier. Also be sure that no part of the plant touches a wall, fence, or adjacent plant that ants could use as a bridge to get around the barrier. Enclosed ant baits such as ant stakes can be placed beneath the plant on the ant trail or near the nest as long as they are inaccessible to young children and pets.

Ants have pincer-like jaws and can bite, but rarely do so. A few ants sting. The California fire ant is the most common stinging ant; it is aggressive and lives mostly outdoors. Red imported fire ants (RIFA) were found in Southern California in 1999. They are very aggressive and each ant can sting several times. RIFA usually make dome-shaped mounds that vary from golf ball to basketball size. They can resemble gopher mounds except that the texture is very fine. If you think you see a RIFA mound, do not disturb it and call the California Department of Food and Agriculture pest hotline at 800-491-1899.

Outdoor ants should be tolerated, except for carpenter ants, which are about one-half inch long, much larger than the Argentine ant. They do not eat wood, but they do hollow it out and nest in it. They may cause considerable damage to buildings as well as trees.

Although outdoor ants may be pests in some situations, they are helpful in other ways such as aerating the soil and helping decompose dead animals and insects. It is unrealistic to try to eliminate ants from an outdoor area and using pesticides for prevention of ant problems is unwise. We expose ourselves and the environment to potential toxic effects and the ants eventually become resistant.

There are three common indoor ants. The Argentine and the odorous house ant (rotten coconut odor when crushed) are both about one-eighth inch long. The pharaoh ant is about one twenty-fifth inch long. It is possible to safely exclude ants from indoor areas. Ants enter buildings seeking shelter during the rainy months and seeking water during hot, dry weather. Indoors, they like to feed on sugary foods, fats and meat. They may appear suddenly if the weather changes or their usual food sources are unavailable.

If you see just a couple of ants on the kitchen counter or floor, kill them and wipe the area with soapy water to remove the scent trail. These are the scouts and they will return with their troops when they find something good to eat.

~ Insects, Pests and Their Control ~

If you see that dreaded, long line of ants in the house, resist the immediate urge to remove them until you trace the line back to its origin. Sometimes you can see the entry point from outside the house when it isn't apparent inside. When you know their entry point, mark it so it can be caulked later. That line of ants can then be quickly and safely removed by vacuuming. The dust in the vacuum kills them. They can also be removed using soapy water and a sponge. Lastly, remove the food source. If you do that first, they will scatter and be harder to remove.

Prevention measures in the kitchen will pay off. Store foods that don't belong in the refrigerator in tightly sealed containers. Likewise, wipe up spills quickly and keep counters and floors clean and dry. If the ants entered because they found water from a leaky faucet or pipe, repair the leak. Look for the entry point and caulk it. If you find other areas where the cracks or holes are larger and dry, diatomaceous earth can be applied in the void before sealing. If ants enter around doors or windows, weather-strip them. Pet food may attract ants, so don't let it sit out for long periods, or put the pet dish in a shallow soapy moat.

Ant baits can be used to get less toxic chemicals into the ant nest. Look for ant baits with boric acid, sulfluramid, hydramethylnon, or arsenic as the active ingredient. Even arsenic baits are safe because they contain very small amounts. They are effective and can be useful when the nest can't be found. After the ant stream has been removed, place the bait in the same spot where the ants had been. The ants are attracted to the bait and carry small amounts of it back to the nest where the entire colony consumes it. Ants won't eat it if more desirable food is available, so good sanitation habits are essential. Baits work over time and may take several weeks to complete the task. Once the ants are gone, remove the bait or it may attract new ants.

Fungus Control for Roses

~

BY JAN SPECHT

If you are not growing roses for competition and simply want lots of lovely blooms for your garden and vase, you may be willing to tolerate less than perfect foliage. Disease-free roses don't exist and sooner or later, everyone will have a problem.

There is no time in the garden where good horticultural care is more important than when growing roses. One reason is that the three most common fungal diseases of roses (powdery mildew, black spot and rust) are difficult to treat, so prevention is worth the effort. Fungi can be spread by wind, soil if the spores are present, improper watering, insects and occasionally by contaminated gardening tools.

Knowing more about the life cycle of these fungi makes it easier to understand why certain gardening practices are important. In its early stage, powdery mildew appears as a whitish covering first seen on the top of the youngest leaves. It likes cool, humid evenings and warm dry days. It over winters in diseased leaves and buds, both on the plant and on the ground. Black spot affects succulent stems and leaves and over winters on canes, infected stems and both living and dead leaves. It causes yellow areas to develop around the spots, and then the entire leaf turns yellow and falls off. It likes temperatures around 75°F and wet leaves, since the spores are spread by splashing water. Rust produces small orange masses mostly on the underside of the leaf. The upper surface discolors and the leaves may drop. Cool, moist weather favors rust. Late in the season, the masses turn black and over winter in leaf and stem tissue.

Whenever possible, consider buying roses that are resistant to these diseases. Visit public rose gardens that match your climate or microclimate, or walk around your neighborhood and notice which

~ *Insects, Pests and Their Control* ~

roses are thriving. Most roses require sun for a minimum of six hours a day. If your garden cannot supply that, the plant is likely to be weak and susceptible to diseases.

The ideal soil for roses is about forty percent compost or other organic matter, twenty percent clay and forty percent sand. This mixture provides adequate water retention and good drainage. Roses should be planted so that the bud union (the grafted area) is slightly above the soil level.

Irrigation practices are critical. When possible, avoid overhead watering so the leaves don't get wet. Overhead watering is often mentioned as a way to decrease powdery mildew, but it could increase the risk of black spot because black spot spores are spread by splashing water. If your irrigation system is an overhead type, time your watering so the leaves can dry in less than seven hours. Black spot requires wet leaves for about seven hours in order to germinate, therefore watering in the early morning is generally best. Avoid splashing soil onto the foliage when watering because there may be spores in the soil from fallen leaves or from over wintering; it may even be necessary to remove some of the lower leaves. Also, routinely monitor the soil for adequate irrigation. Excess water and cool temperatures can contribute to the growth of downy mildew, even harder to control.

Fertilizing roses is necessary, but too much fertilizer causes excessive growth that can interfere with air circulation, increase water needs, result in too much humidity, and encourage aphids.

Appropriate dormant pruning opens up the plant for air circulation and is a good time to remove diseased canes and leaves. Rake the fallen leaves and petals around the roses regularly. It is best not to compost raked debris unless you tend your compost pile regularly and know it is reliably hot. After clean up, apply mulch.

If you use garden tools on an infected plant, it is best to clean them with a diluted bleach solution (one part bleach to nine parts water) after use to prevent transferring the fungus to healthy plants.

When your roses begin to leaf out in spring, it is time to start monitoring for disease every few days. These diseases should be less frequent if your plants are healthy and less severe if you catch them early, when you can remove a few leaves without harming the plant and increase your chance of control. When early signs of the fungus are seen, you may want to spray the rose with one of these less toxic chemicals. Some gardeners spray before signs of disease, but only if weather conditions favor the fungus. They all work better as preventives rather than cures. As with any spray, all solutions should be spot tested on the foliage before general use.

- Baking soda (sodium bicarbonate) has been used as a fungicide for about one hundred years. Mix one tablespoon of baking soda in one gallon of water and then add three tablespoons of horticultural oil.
- Sulfur has also been used as a fungicide for a long time. Use this fungicide according to manufacturer's recommendations. It will burn leaves when temperatures are over 85°F.
- Potassium Dihydrogen Phosphate (PDP) works well for powdery mildew and also acts as a foliar fertilizer. Add one tablespoon to one gallon of water containing one-quarter to one-half teaspoon of liquid detergent.
- Wine vinegar (five percent), but not regular vinegar, has some effect on powdery mildew. Add thirteen tablespoons to one gallon of water. Weekly rotation of the PDP with wine vinegar controlled powdery mildew significantly better than the EPA Class 1 (most toxic) fungicide, Dodemorph.
- Antitranspirants are coatings sprayed onto foliage to prevent water loss. They also create a barrier between the leaf surface and the disease spores, so repeat treatment is needed whenever new growth occurs. Cloud Cover can be used if mixed one part to twelve parts water.
- Neem oil is available commercially as a fungicide but is expensive to use every seven to fourteen days.

Any of these sprays may be used weekly, either alone or in rotation. Experiment in your garden to see what works best for you.

Less Toxic Products and Reading Pesticide Labels

~

BY JAN SPECHT

Less Toxic Products

Faced with shelf upon shelf of garden products at your local nursery or home center, have you ever wondered how to choose the one that will do the least damage to our environment? Luckily, one doesn't have to be a chemist to make some wise choices.

Here are a few of the less toxic items you will find at Bay area nurseries:

- Insecticidal soaps. The active ingredient is potassium salts of fatty acids; it may be the only ingredient, or it can be combined with citrus oil or a chemical called pyrethrin, which is of plant origin. Pyrethrin should not be confused with pyrethroid, which is made from petroleum and can be toxic to beneficial organisms. Insecticidal soaps can be used on aphids, mites, scale, and mealybugs; they must touch the insect's body to be effective, so be sure to apply to undersides of leaves.
- Spray oils (also called horticultural oils or dormant oils). These are highly refined oils that suffocate the target insect. These must also touch the insect's body to be effective.
- Hot pepper spray targets aphids and whiteflies.
- Several different substances can be used to control ants and cockroaches. Borate based products contain boric acid or borax. Hydramethylnon or sulfluramid or fipronil are other choices. Even arsenic ant baits are a less toxic alternative because they contain tiny amounts of arsenic which last a long time.

- An insect growth regulator is available for fleas. Think of methoprene (with or without permethrin) as birth control for fleas. It prevents flea eggs from hatching and inhibits larvae from developing. There is also a borate-based carpet treatment.
- Citrus oil sprays are relatively new on the market. These sprays target ants, cockroaches and indoor fleas, and have the benefit of a pleasant citrus smell.
- Diatomaceous earth products (not the kind used for swimming pools) also control ants, cockroaches and indoor fleas. They absorb the waxy coating on the pest bodies, causing death.
- Neem extract is made from the neem tree. It effectively targets several pests and fungi, but since its release has been found to be toxic to fish, honey bees, and lady bugs. Use sparingly.

All the above names are generic, and for each generic name there are usually several brand or trade names. It's a good idea to get familiar with the generic names, because the trade names often change as new products appear and older ones are taken off the market. Even though these are less toxic products, it is still important to read the entire label and all the instructions on each product. Never use a product unless you are certain that it will work specifically on the pest you've identified. If it is a garden pest, be sure the product can safely be used on the plant. Always follow the recommended procedures for use and disposal.

Even though we are talking about less toxic chemical controls here, these products are still chemicals. Before using any chemical, try non-toxic approaches first, such as hosing off aphids with a strong stream of water, hand picking a small infestation from your plants, encouraging beneficial insects to your garden to help you manage the pests.

~ Insects, Pests and Their Control ~

Reading Pesticide Labels

With good pest management strategies, your need for stronger chemicals should be minimal. However, if you do use a chemical, you must know how to read a pesticide label. Two very toxic pesticides to avoid are diazinon and chlorpyrifos because these are currently contaminating our creeks and Bay. Many garden and household products contain these ingredients.

The label may have two or three names. The most obvious is the brand name but there is also either a common name (for example, diazinon) or a chemical name (the technical name for diazinon) or both. The next item to look for is the active ingredients; these are the chemicals that kill or control the target pest. It is important to read this section because the product may prominently state on the label that (for example) it contains pyrethrins and only mention in the small print under active ingredients that it also contains chlorpyrifos. Inert ingredients are listed just below the active ingredients. The inert ingredients are trade secrets and, with rare exception, by law, do not have to be listed if the label shows them as a percentage of the total material. However, some inerts may be as toxic or more toxic than the active ingredient. Inerts are added for various reasons: to increase potency, to dissolve the pesticide, to prolong its effectiveness, or to increase its ability to adhere to a surface.

The signal words can be anywhere on the label and define the product's acute or immediate toxicity. The word DANGER indicates the pesticide is highly toxic or poses a dangerous health or environmental hazard. Danger may be shown alone or with the word POISON and a skull and crossbones. The word WARNING means moderate toxicity and CAUTION means low toxicity. These signal words give no information about chronic or long-term effects.

Precautionary Statements describe the human and environmental hazards associated with the pesticide. This is an extremely important part of the label because it describes how to avoid exposure and gives information on what kind of protection to use when applying, such as gloves, goggles, mask, long pants and sleeves.

The Directions for Use portion of the label tells how, when and where to use it. It also lists the target pests that the pesticide has been registered to control plus the plant type or other site where it may be used. It may also state plants that are sensitive to the pesticide.

Storage and Disposal information is critical. Never store a hazardous chemical in anything but the original container. The label information is critical to your physician or the emergency services in case of accidental exposure. Unused pesticide should never be disposed of in the trash, poured down a sink or flushed down a toilet. Always read the entire pesticide label before buying, before using, and again before disposing of the pesticide. Take any unused pesticides to your local household hazardous waste collection site.

CHAPTER THIRTEEN

Interactions in the Garden

Insectary Plants Feed Good Bugs

~

by Kathy Reiffenstein

Spring is my favorite time in the garden as green shoots break the surface and vibrant blooms open in the warm sunshine. Unfortunately it also seems to be a favorite time for hungry garden pests, thrilled at the prospect of devouring those juicy young plants. If these 'bad' bugs are left to their own devices, those vibrant blooms may soon be history.

But wait! Before reaching for the pesticide spray, why not enlist Mother Nature's help with the little pests. There are lots of insects that are beneficial in your garden because they are natural predators of the bad guys. Attract ladybugs, lacewings, syrphid flies, tiny parasitic wasps and spiders to your garden and they will feed on aphids, thrips, leafhoppers and cutworms. So, how do you attract these beneficial insects? Add certain plants–known as insectary plants—to your garden to provide food for these good guys. Not only will this help control unwanted guests, it will allow you to virtually eliminate the need to use toxic pesticides.

What plants attract beneficials? Flowering plants that produce lots of pollen and nectar are what they feed on. Since beneficial insects are generally tiny, they like flower heads that are flat and easily accessible, so they don't drown in large, nectar-filled blooms. Consider these insectary plants for your garden:

- Aster (*Aster novi-angliae*)–There are many varieties of this New England Aster, but try 'Purple Dome' which offers a profusion of deep purple flowers with rich green foliage. These bloom in late summer and early fall and are excellent for cutting.
- Baby Blue Eyes (*Nemophila menziesii*)–A California native, this prolific bloomer has sky blue blossoms with a white center. Easily grown in full sun or partial shade, it has a trailing habit, making it a good selection for containers.

~ *Interactions in the Garden* ~

- Coreopsis–There are many species of this easy-to-grow member of the sunflower family, but try *Coreopsis verticillata* 'Moonbeam'. This compact (one to two feet tall) perennial has lacy foliage and soft yellow, star-shaped flowers. Provide full sun and deadhead spent blossoms for continuous bloom well into autumn.
- Coriander (*Coriandrum sativum*)–This is the common herb, cilantro, used in many Mexican and Asian dishes. Delicate fern-like foliage grows twelve to eighteen inches high, perfect for containers or scattered among your perennial beds. Flat clusters of pinkish white flowers appear in summer.
- Erigeron (*Erigeron karvinskianus*)–The Santa Barbara daisy is almost always in bloom, with dainty flower heads made up of many pinkish or white rays. This is a terrific container plant, spilling over the sides and looking lush. Grow in full sun or light shade.
- Feverfew (*Chrysanthemum parthenium*)–This perennial herb has small daisy-like flowers with yellow centers. Grow in full sun for blooms from summer until mid-fall.
- Lavender (*Lavandula augustifolia*)–What garden would be complete without lavender? This is the familiar English lavender, with low growing mounds of foliage. Flower stems rise four to twelve inches above the foliage, topped with spikes of flowers in various shades of purple.
- Queen Anne's Lace (*Daucus carota*)—This is the wild carrot, considered by some to be an invasive weed. So, if you plant it, keep it under control! It needs full sun and when brushed against, gives off an anise-like scent.
- Rudbeckia (*Rudbeckia fulgida sullivantii* 'Goldstrum')–These black-eyed Susans have rough textured, medium green leaves and long stemmed, bright orange-yellow flowers with black "eyes". They're prolific growers and need full sun.
- Sweet Alyssum (*Lobularia maritima*)–A popular annual, this low, trailing plant is frequently seen in rock gardens and

between patio stones. It is fast growing, easily grown from seed and over winters in mild climates like the Bay area. Shear plants back a month after they've bloomed to encourage another burst of flowers.
- Yarrow (*Achillea millefolium*)–Leaves of this perennial are typically gray or grayish green and finely divided. The flower heads are in flattish clusters, ideal for offering up their nectar. Flower colors range from white to pink to yellow, depending on the variety.

Add many different insectary plants to your garden: the more variety of food and shelter you provide, the more types of beneficial insects you'll attract, and the more unwanted pests you'll control.

Good Bugs for Rose Pests

BY JAN SPECHT

Roses can thrive without pesticides in the garden as long as careful attention is given to good horticultural practices. Plant in the proper location so adequate sun is available, water appropriately, don't over fertilize, prune at the right time, and do use mulch. Roses with red or orange flowers are less attractive to pests—a form of control.

Beneficial organisms can be found daily in gardens that are not sprayed with pesticides and that have certain plants to attract them. These insectary plants have clusters of small flowers and include sweet alyssum, yarrow, asters, scabiosa, rosemary, fleabane, dill, coriander and many others, as well as some California native plants. Insectary plants attract beneficial insects by providing nectar and pollen, and a diverse garden has less pest damage. A completely pest free garden is impossible and you will need to tolerate at least a small number of pests from time to time as an invitation for the beneficials.

The following are some common rose pests and some of the least toxic controls, including good bugs, you can use to manage them.

APHIDS

Aphids are the most common arthropod pest of roses. They thrive on new foliage, stems and buds and therefore will be especially numerous on over fertilized plants. Hot summer temperatures will reduce their numbers and a forceful water spray with a hose early in the day can knock them off the plant. You can also prune out the infested areas or use insecticidal soap.

Aphids have several natural enemies. One of the most important is the tiny parasitic wasp. The adult wasp lays eggs in the aphid; the developing wasp kills the aphid, which becomes a dark crusty shell called a mummy. The new wasp then emerges from the mummy through a small round hole. Look for these in your garden with an inexpensive 10-20X hand lens. The parasitic wasp can kill an entire aphid colony in about ten days if you don't kill the wasp with pesticides. This wasp also controls scale, caterpillars and other pests.

Soldier beetles love aphids and are very common on roses. They are predators in the adult and larval stages. Sometimes they leave dark spots of excrement on the leaves and are mistaken for pests. Syrphid flies are also called hover flies because they often hover above flowers. The syrphid larvae are legless, maggot shaped and often found within aphid colonies. Lacewing larvae are a natural enemy of aphids too. The common lady beetle feeds primarily on aphids and is a predator in the adult as well as the larval stage. The larva is about one inch long, alligator shaped and black with orange spots. Be sure not to mistake it for a harmful bug!

Spider Mites

Spider mites are pests that cause pinprick-like, stippled spots on leaves and there may also be webbing on the underside of the leaves. A hand lens is necessary to see them. They are found when the weather is hot and dry and especially if the pesticide carbaryl is used. Periodic overhead watering early in the day can reduce mite numbers. Heavy infestations may require insecticidal soap two or three times per day for several days as well as horticultural oil sprays in late winter to destroy eggs. A number of predatory mites feed on spider mites. Minute pirate bugs are also natural enemies of spider mites.

Scale

Both soft and hard scale attack roses. Badly infested canes can be pruned out to the ground or sprayed every three days for two weeks with a mixture of one tablespoon alcohol per pint of insecticidal soap. Check a small area for phytotoxicity before spraying. Milder cases can be rubbed off with an alcohol soaked cotton swab or nylon scouring pad. Horticultural oil should be applied to canes during the dormant season. Some natural enemies of scale are the tiny parasitic wasp, lady beetles and the minute pirate bug.

Aphids and scale secrete honeydew, which attracts ants and the black sooty mold (a fungus), giving the infestation a dirty appearance. Ants must be controlled before the beneficial insects can work. If you see a ladybug in an aphid colony that has ants, you will notice how the ant chases the ladybug away. Hose off the plant early in the day to remove as many ants as possible. Then apply a double-sided sticky tape to the base of the plant and apply Tanglefoot or Tree Sticky Barrier to the tape. Do not apply these products directly to the plant. Be sure the plant does not touch a fence or potential bridge.

Thrips

Thrips are very small (one twenty-fifth inch long) so a hand lens is helpful to see them. They resemble black or brown slivers of wood. They damage leaves, petals and buds. Thrip problems are worse in late spring and mid-summer and where many rose bushes are located close together. Light colored roses seem to be more attractive to thrips than any other color. Control with sprays is difficult because this pest resides deep within the blossom. However, lacewings, minute pirate bugs and predatory mites all prey on thrips and are quite effective. Beneficial nematodes can kill thrips in the pupal stage in the soil.

Leafhoppers

Roses are the food source for only one of the several annual generations of the leafhopper insect. The immature forms of the other generations feed on oaks, elms and other plants. The eggs are deposited in fall within the bark of rose, raspberry and blackberry canes and look like small, dark, raised spots. Directly spraying the adults with insecticidal soap or neem oil will control them. Spray during cool morning or evening temperatures when they don't move quickly. Sticky rolls of commercially available tape or traps are also effective. The parasitic wasp egg, available commercially, can reduce populations enough so that other control measures are not necessary.

Diversity in the Garden

by Nancy Bauer

Healthy plants, just like healthy bodies, are more resistant to disease. Like people, plants need a nutritious diet. A soil rich in microorganisms, organic matter and minerals provides healthy plant food. Plants also need, of course, the right amount of sun or shade and water. But what about attacks from insect pests? While a healthy plant is less attractive to insects, it needs a little support from its friends.

To keep insect pests from gaining the upper ground, there must be beneficial insects and other predators around. To attract them to the garden, we plant a wide variety of plants, which creates an ecosystem of prey and predator that helps maintain a healthy balance in the garden. Nectar flowers bring hummingbirds, bees, butterflies, and other pollinators. Plants that provide food and shelter for birds and other beneficials offer seeds, berries or nuts, pollen, and nectar. A wren, for example, can consume more than five hundred insect eggs, beetles, and grubs in one afternoon! Other beneficials such as garden spiders, lacewings, dragonflies, soldier bugs, and ground beetles also feed on insect pests. By growing in healthy soil and planting a variety of food and nectar plants, the focus automatically changes to prevention, rather than intervention. When that happens, a more positive and creative energy seems to flow into the garden.

Native plants and local insects have depended on each other for their survival for a long time. Take advantage of this relationship by planting native trees, shrubs, vines, flowers and grasses. Blue elderberry, ceanothus, coffeeberry, toyon, and native viburnums attract beneficial insects and birds and look good in the landscape over a long period of time. Native mallows, asters, salvias, buckwheats and yarrow attract pollinators and insect predators.

~ Interactions in the Garden ~

Members of the sunflower family (cosmos, yarrow, feverfew, Gloriosa daisy, zinnia, marigold) are highly favored food plants of many beneficial insects. Grow tasty insect plants of the umbellifer family (carrots, fennel, parsley, dill, angelica, Queen Anne's lace, lovage, bishop flower), especially near the vegetable garden. They'll attract beneficial insects and provide a few edibles for the kitchen, too. Because many herbs both attract beneficials and repel insect pests, they make perfect companions for ornamentals and vegetables. Sage, thyme, garlic, oregano, tansy, rosemary and mint, for example, protect neighboring plants with their strong scents. Their flower nectar brings in the pollinators and other beneficials. Sweet alyssum is an excellent beneficial insect plant as a border around roses and other ornamentals.

If you spray, you may kill a few of the pests, but you will kill the larger and more susceptible beneficial insects as well. Then you risk an outbreak of many pests, who no longer have predators to keep them in check. Consider a few imperfect leaves a small price to pay for a pesticide free garden. Aphids, for example, can be washed off, but they are also the favorite food supply of the ladybug. Bugs are messengers. They attack weak and stressed plants. Observe your plants. Is this plant happy where it is? Does it need less water? More shade? Are you feeding the soil, instead of the plant? Take a closer look.

Which insects are beneficial and which are pests is a judgment call we make from our own narrow perspective. In the big picture of insect and plant relationships, these distinctions are not so clear. A friend who had been feeding the "brown pests" in her snapdragons to resident birds was horrified to discover that they were the caterpillars of the handsome Buckeye butterfly. Snapdragons are one of several caterpillar food plants of the Buckeye, and though they may be pruned by the few caterpillars that survive their predators, they will not be destroyed. Just to be safe, though, my friend now plants a few extra.

Plants as Pollution Cleansers

~

by Diane Lynch

We think of plants having value to us because they are beautiful and useful, providing food and medicine as well as contributing oxygen to the atmosphere. But scientists all over the world are currently studying and using plants to remove many types of water and soil pollution. The process is called phytoremediation, a word coined by Dr. Ilya Raskin, professor of plant biology at Rutgers, who used sunflowers to mop up radioactive waste in a pond near the Chernobyl nuclear power plants. Grown on styrofoam rafts, the flowers soaked up cesium and strontium at levels several thousand times higher than the concentration in the contaminated pond.

Phytoremediation (phyto means plant) is the use of living plants to clean up, or remediate, soil, ground water, sludges or sediments by removing pollutants. Some plants can degrade organic pollutants or function as filters or traps for metals. Phytoremediation has been used to clean up metals, pesticides, solvents, explosives, crude oil, polyaromatic hydrocarbons and landfill leachates. Generally these techniques work best on sites with low to medium levels of contamination in shallow soils, streams and ground water.

Places contaminated with metals can be cleaned up by using plants, called hyperaccumulators, that absorb large quantities of metals. These plants, such as Indian mustard, cottonwood, hybrid poplar and certain grasses, are planted, allowed to grow for some time and then harvested, after which they are either incinerated or composted to recycle the metals. When incinerated, the ash will amount to less than ten percent of the volume of contaminated soil. There are about four hundred plants known to capture metals in this way. Nickel, for example, is extracted from soil by moving up into plant roots, stems and leaves. After the plant is harvested, the site is replanted until the nickel recedes to acceptable levels. Scientists at the University of Florida have discovered that brake fern, native to the southeast, accumulates arsenic at levels as high as two hundred times the surrounding contaminated soil at a lumberyard. Imagine the possibilities of mining various metals using plants.

Chevron is using cattails to extract selenium emitted from its Point Richmond refinery. Some of the selenium captured by the cattails is excreted into the air at nontoxic levels. The cattails can be harvested and spread over soil that is deficient in the metal or disposed of. Selenium is a naturally occurring, necessary nutrient, but in agricultural areas it can accumulate at toxic levels in water and harm wildlife and livestock. This process should cost a fraction of what it would cost to dredge and dispose of the sediments, according to University of California (UC) Berkeley plant biologist Norman Terry. Dr. Terry has also experimented with broccoli, rice and cabbage to clean up selenium contaminated soil and found that they also have the ability to absorb the metal and convert it to a nontoxic gas, dimethyl selenide, which disperses into the atmosphere. Recent tests have shown that pickleweed, a common native salt marsh plant, is better at removing selenium than any other plant tested. It shows promise at helping clean up San Joaquin Valley agricultural runoff.

Organic pollutants (those with carbon and hydrogen atoms) can be remediated in a couple of ways. Plants produce enzymes (proteins) that can break down some pollutants. Also, contaminants can be broken down by microbial activity of such microorganisms as yeast, fungi and bacteria, which occur around the root zone of the plant. Former ammunition sites have been treated with water plants such as duckweed and parrotfeather. Hybrid poplar and eastern cottonwood take up chlorinated solvents, which degrade into simpler molecules and are incorporated into the plant.

Wetlands have enormous value, providing flood, erosion, pollution and sediment control as well as essential habitat for diverse types of wildlife and forming the basis of a complex food web. We in the

Bay area live near the most extensive salt marshes of the western coastal states. Beyond the obvious value of wetlands, there have been successful studies where artificial wetlands planted with parrotfeather, a common aquatic weed, have cleaned up water beneath old military firing ranges. The Point Richmond refinery wetlands provide habitat for wildlife as they take up selenium. Some plants and trees such as poplars can suck up large quantities of water and give off pollutants as the water passes out of the plant. This can prevent surface contaminants from moving into ground water. This can be exploited to benefit riparian zones by preventing the spread of such pollution.

Current research at UC Berkeley and other institutions is focused on genetic manipulation, as scientists attempt to accumulate the best features of plants, as well as bacteria and other life forms, which will help us clean up some of the messes we've made. Julian Schroeder, a biologist at UC San Diego, says large plants such as trees can have the necessary genes inserted to allow them to absorb larger quantities of specific toxins. Despite widespread public skepticism, the possibilities for using these powerful tools in a constructive, safe manner are being studied and good uses are already being discovered.

The possibilities for cleaning up pollution are vast as we learn to harness the power of plants to decontaminate toxic sites. There are thousands of sites that need cleaning, and growing plants to clean them up will be cheaper and far less invasive, inconvenient and dirty than the fleets of dump trucks and other methods currently used.

Bay Area Gardens to Visit

by Maggie Agro

MARIN ART AND GARDEN CENTER, a ten-acre site in the center of Marin County, is working to become the county horticultural center. With the efforts of member garden clubs and Marin Master Gardeners, this well-contained garden center will soon offer demonstration gardens and workshops. Visit shops and an art gallery or take part in some of the activities sponsored by one of the many founding and affiliate groups. 30 Sir Francis Drake Blvd., Ross. 415-454-5597. Open dawn to dusk. Free.

LUTHER BURBANK HOME AND GARDENS is a living outdoor museum featuring Luther Burbank's work, including many of the plants he developed during his lifetime. In over one acre of gardens, you can view medicinal herbs, a wildlife habitat, gardens that feature plants popular in the late 1800's, and enjoy cutting gardens, demonstration beds, fruit trees and much more. There is very good signage, with both common and botanical names. Santa Rosa at Sonoma Avenue, Santa Rosa. 707-524-5445. Gardens open daily year round, 8am to dusk, no charge; tours of home, greenhouse and a portion of the garden, 10am to 3:30pm, April through October, Tuesday through Sunday, fees $3 for adults and free for children under 12. Call to arrange tours for groups. http://ci.santa-rosa.ca.us/rp/burbank/

QUARRYHILL BOTANICAL GARDEN, on 40 acres of rolling hills above Sonoma Valley, houses one of the largest collections of scientifically documented wild-source Asian plants in North America. Glen Ellen. 707-996-3802. Open by appointment only March through October. Docent-led study tours available by reservation only. Free, donations encouraged.

NATIVE PLANTS GARDEN, Sonoma State University is a four-acre arboretum created to showcase California's major plant communities. Take a self-guided nature trail and view the major species within each plant community. Includes an extensive butterfly garden. 1801 Cotati Avenue, Rohnert Park. 707-664-2103. Open dawn to dusk. Free.

SONOMA HORTICULTURAL NURSERY, famous for its lush display of rhododendrons and azaleas in early spring, is a natural 7-acre woodland setting with flowering plants of all types for shade. You'll find unusual plants and gorgeous color in this collector's paradise. 3970 Azalea Avenue, Sebastopol. 707-823-6832. 9am to 5pm, every day, March through May. Closed Tuesday and Wednesday the rest of the year. Nonguided or guided tours for groups of ten or fewer are free. $3 fee per person for larger groups includes a $2 voucher toward plant purchase. http://www.sonomahort.com

WESTERN HILLS NURSERY, a working nursery well known in the horticultural community, is equally appealing to both the experienced and novice gardener. Enjoy the garden's natural setting with paths, bridges and hidden vistas and plants of every hue, size, and form. Plants available for purchase. 16250 Coleman Valley Road, Occidental. 707-874-3731. Open February through November, Thursday through Sunday, 10am to 4pm. No tours. No fee.

In San Francisco, GOLDEN GATE PARK hosts a plethora of garden experiences including the Rose Garden, the Queen Wilhelmina Tulip Garden and windmills, and the Aids Memorial Grove. 415-831-2700. Open sunrise to sunset. Free. Visit the Japanese Tea Garden from 8:30am to 6:00pm. Admission is $3.50 for adults, $1.25 for children 6-12 and seniors.

While in Golden Gate Park, leave time to tour STRYBING ARBORETUM AND BOTANICAL GARDENS to enjoy one of the world's finest botanical gardens and arboretums. Its 55 acres contain plants from the world's Mediterranean climates to high-elevation tropical cloud forests. 9th Avenue at Lincoln Way (Golden Gate Park). 415-661-1316. Open 365 days a year, weekdays 8am to 4:30pm, 10am-5pm weekends and holidays. Free, donation encouraged. Call for docent-led Strybing walking tour schedule. For Strybing's special spring garden tour/workshops in Marin, the East Bay and Peninsula, dial Ext 354. http://www.strybing.org/

In the East Bay, visit BERKELEY MUNICIPAL ROSE GARDEN to see over 3,000 different roses and its innovative garden design. Tucked into a quiet north-side Berkeley neighborhood, a highlight is the rose amphitheater with tiers of different-colored roses. Blooms May-September. 1201 Euclid Avenue at Bay View Place, Berkeley. 510-644-6530. Open daily 7am to10pm. Free.

An excellent example of a Mediterranean garden, 10.5 acre BLAKE GARDEN is a teaching facility that reflects Italian and Asian influences, as well as more contemporary design. The setting for the residence of the UC Berkeley president, you will enjoy seeing the garden in the context of this stately home. 70 Rincon Road, Kensington. 510-524-2449. Open 8am to 4:30pm, Monday to Friday. Free. Tours available for groups of ten or more, by reservation only.

~ Bay Area Gardens to Visit ~

DUNSMUIR HOUSE AND GARDEN, an historic house and 50-acre estate, is open each year from April to September. Three different routes are included in the self-guided landscape tour of the estate grounds. Trees and other plant material are well marked and described in the tour booklet. 2960 Peralta Oaks Court, Oakland. 510-615-5555. Tuesday through Friday, 10 am to 4 pm, free. Call for weekend tour rates and times.

EAST BAY REGIONAL PARKS BOTANIC GARDEN, located in Tilden Regional Park, is devoted to the preservation of native plants. The Garden is divided into ten sections and three subsections, each representing a distinctive natural area of California. You can see plants growing in their natural habitat with their natural companions. Signage provides the common name, scientific name, family name, endangerment status of a plant, and when and where it was collected. Good resource for the novice gardener or anyone who wants to learn more about gardening with natives. Wildcat Canyon Road and South Park Drive, Berkeley. 510-841-8732. Open daily 8:30am to 5pm. Garden tours at 2:00pm on Saturdays and Sundays. Free. http://www.nativeplants.org/

LAKESIDE PARK GARDEN CENTER, part of the large park complex that fronts Lake Merritt, is home to the Golden State Bonsai Collection, palmatum, cactus and succulents and demonstration composting gardens. 666 Bellevue Avenue, Oakland, 510-238-3208. Bonsai garden open weekdays 10am to 3pm, Saturdays and Sunday from 10am to 5pm. Winter hours (November to April) are 10am to 4pm all days. Free.

To view a beautifully designed oasis in an urban setting, visit KAISER CENTER ROOF GARDEN, 3.5 acres of ornamental trees, shrubs and perennials atop the Kaiser Center Garage. At the corner of Harrison and 20th, or you may want to ask for directions to the entrance at the information kiosk at 300 Lakeside Drive, Oakland. 510-271-6197. Open Monday-Friday, 7am to 7pm, admission is free. Tours are available, but must call for reservations. Enjoy the noon concert series on Fridays from June through September.

Oakland's official rose garden, MORCOM AMPHITHEATER OF ROSES, is a walk through a fantasyland of roses and columned terraces. This classic Italian-style garden setting reaches its peak bloom in mid-May. Known for its collection of modern hybrid tea roses, the garden is an excellent place to see over 500 All-American rose selections and a collection of historic hybrid teas from the 1920's to the 1950's. 700 Jean Street, Oakland. 510-238-3187. Open daily dawn to dusk. Free.

The NILES ROSE GARDEN, on the one acre historic California nursery in Fremont, was renovated and is maintained by the Friends of Heirloom Flowers. In addition to 500 roses, you'll also find a vegetable garden for the hungry and a butterfly perennial garden. 36501 Niles Blvd. at Nursery Blvd., Fremont, 9:30am - 4:30pm every day but Tuesdays. 510-656-7702. No fee, picnicking and pets welcome.

SHINN HISTORICAL PARK AND ARBORETUM is a Victorian ranch house, surrounded by 4.5 acres of grounds. First planted as a nursery by the Shinn family in the 1870's, the house and gardens is a popular site for gardeners and tree lovers who come to see the many unusual specimen trees. Sydney Street, off Peralta Blvd, Fremont. 510-791-4340. Open daily, sunrise to one hour after sunset. Tours of the house are available by calling 510-795-0891.

UC BOTANICAL GARDEN, with 34 acres above the Berkeley campus, is the fifth-largest botanical garden in the world. Too large to absorb during any one visit, it contains 13,000 species and 21,000 plants by region and a large collection of rare and endangered species. This living museum and major center for plant research, display and education is worth several visits during each season. 200 Centennial Drive, Berkeley. 510-643-2755. Open daily except Christmas, 9am to 5pm; extended to 7pm from Memorial Day to Labor Day. Fees: Thursdays free. All other days: Adults $3, seniors $2, children 3 - 18 $1, UC students free. http://www.mip.berkeley.edu/garden/

THE GARDENS AT HEATHER FARM is a non-profit five-acre complex with a greenhouse, lath house, community building and three acres of demonstration gardens with plant materials suited to a Mediterranean climate. 1540 Marchbanks Drive, Walnut Creek. 925-947-1678. Open weekdays, sunrise to sunset. Free. Nominal fee for group tours.

LINDSAY MUSEUM NATURE GARDEN, focusing on living with nature, is a wildlife rehabilitation and natural history center that exhibits some non-releasable native wildlife in a natural setting. The Nature Garden surrounding the museum features native plantings with oak woodlands, meadows, chaparral and many annuals and perennials. 1931 First Avenue, Walnut Creek. 925-935-1978. Open daily dawn to dusk. Garden is free. Call for museum hours and fee.

MARKHAM REGIONAL ARBORETUM, 16 acres in the heart of Concord, is a developing garden sanctuary in the middle of an urban community. Their International Garden allows you to see trees from all over the world that work well in our Mediterranean climate. Participate in a free propagation workshop every Tuesday from 9am until noon. 1202 La Vista Avenue, Concord. 925-681-2968. Gardens are open daily from 8 am until dark. Free.

~ Bay Area Gardens to Visit ~

Visit RUTH BANCROFT GARDEN to see a rich collection of desert and dry climate plants and their integration into well-planned landscape design. 1500 Bancroft Rd, Walnut Creek. 925-210-9663. $5 fee for garden tours. Call for schedule of guided tours and events. Reservations required. Plant sales after each tour.

Travel down the Peninsula to ALLIED ARTS GUILD, a community of Spanish-Colonial style buildings that play host to working artists and shops for visitors. The 3.5-acre complex, inspired by gardens in Granada, Spain, feature Spanish-style Mediterranean arches, fountains, and courtyards nestled among the many buildings. The center benefits Lucille Salter Packard Children's Hospital at Stanford. 75 Arbor Road, Menlo Park. 650-325-3259. Open Monday through Saturday, 10 to 5. No fee.

FILOLI, one of America's great garden estates, is set on 654 acres with native oaks, wetlands and a 16-acre formal garden. While beautiful at any time, many enjoy Filoli's numerous orchid specimens and floral arrangements from the garden displayed in the house during blooming season. 86 Canada Road, Woodside. 650-364-8300. Open February 13 – October 27, 2001 from 10am to 3pm, Tuesday through Saturday. Adults $10, children 2-12 $1. Map provided for self-guided tours and volunteers are available to answer questions. Reservations required for two-hour docent-led tours of house and garden or for 2.5 hour guided nature walks. http://www.filoli.org

To experience a traditional Japanese tea garden, visit the JAPANESE TEA GARDEN at Central Park, San Mateo, where you can view a koi pond, waterfall, a teahouse, Japanese shinden or shrine, Turtle Island, and many Japanese plants and trees suitable for our climate. A joint effort of San Mateo, its Japanese-American and gardening communities, and its sister city, Toyonaka, Japan, this garden was designed by Nagao Sakurai, Imperial Palace architect. Plan to come at noon for the koi feeding or let your children enjoy a train ride nearby in the park. 50 West 5th Avenue, San Mateo. 650-522-7420. Open weekdays 10am to 4pm, weekends 11am to 4pm. No fee.

If you've consulted the *Sunset Western Garden Book*, you'll appreciate the DEMONSTRATION GARDENS laid out to match the Sunset garden zones that run from the Pacific Northwest to the Mexican desert at SUNSET PUBLISHING CORPORATION HEADQUARTERS in Menlo Park. You can see plants for the various zones and you'll also find many examples that work in your own garden setting. 80 Willow Road, Menlo Park. 650-321-3600. Open Monday - Friday 9am to 4:30pm. Free. Map available for self-guided tours. No reservations required for groups of ten or less.

Author Biographies

~

MAGGIE AGRO, on the Board of the Marin Master Gardeners, is a water media artist and print maker. She is also a member of the Marin Society of Artists and a freelance writer. Her works have been shown, and published, throughout the Bay area.

NANCY BAUER is a writer, garden columnist, and author of *The Habitat Garden Book: Wildlife Landscaping for the San Francisco Bay Region*.

JULIE WARD CARTER was President of the Marin Master Gardeners in 2000-2001 and is currently the Integrated Pest Management Coordinator and workshop leader for the Master Gardeners. In her spare time, she continually expands her acre plus garden at her home in San Rafael.

M.C. DWYER began gardening when she was eight years old, when her family moved to the California foothills and planted a one acre garden brimming with fresh flowers, ripe vegetables and thorny berries. In college, she hauled her healthy houseplants home every summer in the back of a Chevy pickup. M.C. hopes to continue sharing her love of plants and nature with others, at least into her eighties, carrying on a long family tradition.

BARBARA J. EUSER savors morning in her hillside garden before she starts writing. She is the author of *Take 'Em Along: Sharing the Wilderness with Your Children* and co-author of *A Climber's Climber: On the Trail with Carl Blaurock*. She was managing editor of the *Solar Law Reporter* and a contributing editor of *Passionfruit: A Women's Travel Journal*. Her essays have appeared in magazines and anthologies.

ELIZABETH NAVAS FINLEY is a Master Gardener who was inspired by her training to become a garden designer after two decades spent writing on landscaping for newspapers and magazines.

VIRGINIA HAVEL is a longtime home gardener in Inverness. She is a retired biology teacher at the College of Marin, a founder of the Environmental Forum of Marin, and an active member of the California Native Plant Society. Her special interests are gardening with native plants and controlling exotic pest plants in natural landscapes.

~ Author Biographies ~

I'LEE HOOKER has been a Master Gardener since 1999. She used to be a ceramic artist and now is an avid gardener. Her garden has been published in various magazines. She has written garden articles for the *Marin Independent Journal* and currently writes a gardening column for her local Tiburon newspaper, *The Ark*.

TERUMI LEINOW, a Certified Feng Shui Consultant and Master Gardener, feels passionate about both. She is a popular greater Bay area consultant, teacher and speaker, as she has a unique ability to make the esoteric art of feng shui understandable, practical, useable and fun.

DIANE LYNCh originally trained as a Master Gardener in Dallas and is currently serving as Community Service co-chair for the Marin Master Gardeners as well as writing gardening articles for two local newspapers. In her spare time, she tends an ornamental garden heavy on habitat plants in Tiburon and a mixed orchard and vegetable garden in Freestone.

STACY NELSON is a member of the Marin Master Gardeners, a Trustee of Marin Art and Garden Center and principal of Stacy Nelson Design Concepts, a home and garden design firm. Stacy has written and published various articles about Bay area gardening. Her design work has been written about in newspapers, has gained a spot on the Channel 4 news and is being featured in a national home and garden magazine.

LEE OLIPHANT, a Master Gardener, is an educator who writes for professional publications. Her real love is gardening; specializing in deer and drought resistant landscaping and kitchen gardens.

KATHY REIFFENSTEIN, 2001-2 President of the Marin Master Gardeners, has over 80 containers in her waterfront garden in Mill Valley. In addition to writing gardening articles for various publications, she is the Contributing Editor for Container Gardening at *Suite101.com* and gives slide presentations and workshops on container gardening and garden design.

JAN SPECHT has two diverse gardens. The easy one is the container garden on the decks around the house and the challenging one is a steep, dry hillside with deer. She uses Integrated Pest Management principles for both and organic methods for the edibles. Mother Nature surely appreciates her efforts.

Index

Abies spp., 10
Abiotic disorders, 50-51
Acacia, 10, 21, 157, 158
Acer spp., 11
Achilleas, 5, 81, 103-105, 124, 136, 190
Acid soil, 101
Acidity, 27, 47
Adenostoma fasciculatum., 10
Adiantum jordanii, 30
Aeonium urbicum, 15
Aeration, 48, 63
Aesculus californica., 11
Africa, 20
African violet, 154
Agapanthus spp., 11, 21, 62. 64
Agastache foeniculum, 73
Air circulation, 25, 27
Air pollution, 50
Alders, 11
Alfalfa pellets, 63
Algae, 48
Algeria, 22, 96
Alkalinity, 27, 47, 51
Allelopath, 143
Almonds, 22
Alnus spp., 11
Aloes, 11, 83
Aloysia triphylla, 73
Alstroemeria 21, 134
Aluminum sulfate, 102
Aluminum, 101
Alyssum, 80, 195
Amending soil, 62, 36
Ammonia odor in compost, 44
Anemone, Japanese, 158
Anethum graveolens, 5
Angelica, 195
Anise hyssop, 73
Annuals, 58, 77
Antitranspirants, 182
Ants, 163, 177-179
Aphids, 48, 54, 78, 96, 191, 193

Apple, 13
Arachnids, 172
Arctostaphylos, 11, 93, 133, 134
Armeria maritima, 124
Armillaria, 50
Arsenic, 197
Artemesia, 10, 58, 81, 124
Artichokes, 22, 54
Asarum caudatum, 144
Asclepsias, 88, 149
Asexual reproduction, 152
Asparagus, 22
Asters, 58, 77, 88, 188, 194
Athyrium felix-femina, 130
Australia, 20, 21
Azalea, 47, 60, 62, 63, 145
Aztec sweet, 73
Baby Blue Eyes, 188
Baccharis, 10
Bacteria, 2, 33, 48, 50
Bait, ant, 178
Bait, slug and snail, 176
Baking soda, 182
Balkan peninsula, 22
Bamboo, 10, 115, 158
Bambusa spp., 10
Baneberry, 28
Barberry, 15, 153
Bark chips, 63
Barley, 22
Basil, 54
Bay trees, 10, 29, 54
Beans, 22, 54, 151
Bees, 136, 163-165
Beetles, 54, 85, 192
Beets, 59, 66
Begonia, 53, 63, 154
Bellflowers, 58
Beneficial insects, 4, 5, 59, 78, 184, 188, 194-195
Beneficial microorganisms, 46, 48, 49
Beneficial organisms, 2, 166, 170, 173, 177, 191
Berberis, 15

~ Index ~

Berkeley Botanical Gardens, 107
Bermuda grass, 65
Biennials, 65, 86
Billbug, 120
Bird's foot fern, 30
Birds, 85, 89-91, 92-93, 132, 134, 136, 157, 164, 194
Bishop's cap, 28
Black sage, 10
Black Sect Tantric Buddhism (BTB), 13
Black spot, 54, 180
Blackberry, Himalayan, 157
Black-eyed Susans, 77
Blechnum spicant, 130
Bloodroot, 28
Blue dicks, 61
Bluebells, 59
Bluegrass, 65
Borers, 56
Boron, micronutrient, 46
Bottlebrush, 21
Bougainvillea, 62
Bouteloua gracilis, 116
Bracken fern, 30
Broccoli, 53, 59, 66, 197
Brodiaea, 60, 61
Broom, 10, 157, 158, 159
Buckeye butterfly, 88
Buckeye, 11, 88
Buckwheat, 194
Buddleia spp., 11
Bulbs, 59, 77, 112, 147
Bunch grasses, 88
Butterflies, 59, 86, 87-88, 133, 194, 195
Butterflies-in-the-wind, 125
Butterfly bush, 11
Butterfly weed, 149
Cabbage, 22, 58, 59, 66, 197
Cabbageworms, 54
Cactus, 126-128
Calcium, secondary nutrient, 46, 47
Calendula, 54, 74, 83
California Native Plant Society, 92
California natives, 10, 20, 29, 31, 59, 60-61, 65, 90, 92-93
Calla lily, 21, 58, 59
Callistemon spp., 21
Calochortus, 60
Calypso bulbosa, 110

Camellias, 51, 62. 63
Campanula, 58
Canada, 89
Canterbury bells, 65
Carbaryl, 192
Carex, 88, 116
Carmel creeper, 124
Carrots, 59, 86
Caterpillar, 87-88, 90
Catmint, 136
Cattail, 116, 197
Cattleya, 110, 111
Cauliflower, 59
Ceanothus, 5, 11, 54, 88, 90, 93, 124, 133, 135, 194
Cedars, 10, 158
Celery, 53
Centranthus ruber, 161
Chamise, 10
Chaparral, 61
Checkerbloom, 88
Chemical fertilizer, 33
Cherry, 62, 92, 153
Chi, 12
Chick peas, 22
Chile, 20, 21
Chinch bugs, 120
Chinese gardens, 13
Chlorine, micronutrient, 46
Chlorophyll, 28
Chlorpyrifos, 185
Chrysanthemum parthenium, 189
Cistus spp. , 11, 22
Clay soil, 33-35, 42, 63
Clematis, 154
Clintonia, 145
Clones, 152
Clover, 87
Cocoa bean hulls, 40
Cocoa, 63
Coffeeberry, 90, 92, 133, 145, 194
Coleus, 154
Compost, 3, 26, 35, 38, 39, 42-45, 63, 65, 119, 149, 170
Coneflower, 53
Conifer, 21
Container gardening, 75-80, 142
Convolvulus, 77
Copper strips, 175

Copper, micronutrient, 46, 47
Coral bells, see Heuchera, 58, 98-99, 134
Corallorhiza, 110
Coreopsis, 53, 54, 62, 77, 88, 189
Coriander, 5, 189
Corms, 60, 147
Corn gluten, 120
Corn, 22
Cornus nuttalli, 11
Correa, 133
Corsica, 95
Cortaderia spp, 10
Cosmos, 5, 80, 88, 195
Cotoneaster, 11, 158
Cottonseed meal, 63
Cottonwood, 196
Coyote brush, 10
Cranes bill geraniums, 95
Crassulas, 154
Crocus, 58
Crown rot, 30
Currant, 90, 93, 133, 153
Cuttings, 152-154
Cutworm, 120
Cyclamen spp., 22
Cymbidium, 110, 149
Cymbopogon citralus, 73
Cyperus, 116
Cypripedium californicum, 110
Cytisus, 10, 153
Dactylis glomerata 'Variegata', 116
Daffodils, 22, 54, 58, 59, 64, 66
Dahlias, 53, 63
Daisies, 21, 53, 58, 158
Damping-off, 53
Daucus carota, 189
Daylily, 58, 64, 136, 148
Deadheading, 80, 158
Deadwood, removal of, 3, 57, 66
Decaying matter, 26
Deciduous oaks, 67, 69
Decomposition, 42, 46
Deer resistant plants, 81
Defoliation, 38
Diatomaceous earth, 175, 179, 184
Diazinon, 185
Dichelostemmas, 61
Dictamnus, 149

Dietes, 124
Dill, 5, 80, 86
Dinosaur food, 21
Discolored foliage, 50
Disease problems, 48, 96
Diseased wood, removal of, 57
Dividing plants, 58, 148-149
Douglas iris, 60
Dracaena, 153
Drainage, 35, 48
Drought tolerant ferns, 29-31
Drought tolerant plants, 14, 20, 54, 88
Dutch iris, 59
Dutchman's breeches, 28
Dutchman's pipe, 87, 88
Earthworms, 2, 36, 40, 45, 48, 49
Echeveria, 15
Echinacea, 81, 82
Ecosystem, 86, 93
Egypt, 22
Elderberry, 90, 93, 133, 194
Epilobium canum (Zauschneria californica), 11, 86, 133, 160
Epipactis gigantea, 110
Equisetum, 116
Erica, 153
Erigeron karvinskianus, 136, 161, 189
Erosion, 36, 48, 49
Escallonia spp., 11
Escheveria spp., 11
Ethylene gas, 59
Eucalyptus, 10, 21, 156, 157
Europe, 22
Evening primrose, 86
Fabric, horticultural, 175
Fairy lanterns, 60
Fall planting, 58, 60-61
False Lily-of-the-valley, 145
False Solomon's Seal, 145
FAO, 150
Feng shui, 12-13
Fennel, 5, 86, 87, 88
Ferns, 29-31, 60, 62, 129-130, 134, 143, 197
Fertilizer, 33, 46-49, 63, 76, 78, 117, 118, 121, 170, 181
Fescue, 65, 116, 117
Feverfew, 82, 98, 189, 195
Fiery skipper, 120

~ Index ~

Fig, 22, 153
Fir bark mulch, 63
Fire hazard, 39
Firecracker flower, 61
Fire-resistant plants, 9-11
Firs, 10
Flammables, 9-11, 37, 39
Flax, New Zealand, 116
Flies, 44
Flies, syrphid, 191
Flycatcher, 90
Foeniculum vulgare, 5
Foliage, 38, 50, 51
Food and Agriculture Organization, 150
Forest, 42, 89
Forget-me-nots, 58
Forsythia, 153
Fragaria californica, 136, 160
France, 96
Freesias, 59
Fried egg plant, 134
Fringed bleeding heart, 28
Fronds, 30
Frost, 50
Fruit trees, 55, 62, 64, 67
Fuchsias, 21, 62, 106-108, 133, 153, 160
Fungicide, 99, 171
Fungus, 2, 25, 33, 36, 48, 50, 56, 86, 144, 152, 170, 180-182, 184
Gama, blue, 116
Garlic, 54, 59
Gas plant, 149
Gaura, 125
Gazania, 158
Genetic diversity, 150
Geranium, 11, 28, 62, 93, 153
German chamomile, 73
Gibbons, Euell, 105
Ginger, wild or long-tailed, 28, 144
Gladiolus spp., 21, 53, 64
Globe tulip, 60
Gnatcatcher, blue-gray, 90
Goldenrod, 88
Golueke, Clarence, 42
Goodyera oblongifolia, 110
Gooseberry, 93, 133
Gorse, 157
Grape hyacinth, 59

Grape, 22, 153, 154
Grass, lawn, 117-120
Grasses, 77, 115-116, 117, 134, 148, 157-159, 196
Grasslands, 61, 89
Great Petaluma Desert Nursery, 127
Greenhouse, 16,-18, 152
Grevillea, 21, 133, 136
Grosbeak, 85
Ground cover, 117, 121-122
Growth-regulating hormone, 152
Grubs, white 120
Guelph, University of, 97
Gunnera, 21
Habitat gardening, 85-88, 89-91, 92-93
Heading cuts, 56, 67
Heartsease, 83
Heavy metals, micronutrients, 46
Hebe, 15
Hedges, 62
Heims, Dan, 98
Helianthus, 5
Helichrysum petiolare, 77, 98
Helix aspera, 174
Hemerocallis, 134, 136
Hens & chicks, 11, 15
Herbicide, 37, 117, 120
Herbs, 77, 79, 81-83, 88, 195
Heteromeles arbutifolia, 11, 92
Heuchera, 11, 98-99, 134, 135
Hollyhocks, 65, 147
Honeydew, 170
Honeysuckle, 154, 157
Hormone, growth-regulating, 152
Hormone, rooting, 153, 154
Hornets, 163
Horsetail, 116
Host plants, 87, 88
Howe, Lyn, 85
Huckleberry, 145
Hummingbirds, 90, 92, 93, 133, 136, 160, 194
Humus, 26, 27
Hyacinths, 58, 61
Hybrid plants, 151
Hydrangeas, 13, 69, 100-102, 153
Hymenoptera, 163
Hyperaccumulators, 196-198
Hypericum, 81, 82
Ice plant, 11, 158

Iceland poppies, 58
Insectary plants, 5, 188-190, 191
Insecticide, 120
Insectivores, 85
Insects, 39, 50
Insects, beneficial, 194-195
Insects, predator, 194-195
Inside-out flower, 145
Integrated Pest Management (IPM), 5
Invasive plants, 156-158, 159-160
IPM, 5
Ipomoea 'Margarite', 98
Iris, 11, 22, 28, 58, 59, 60, 64, 124, 132, 136,156
Irish potato famine, 150
Iron, micronutrient, 46, 47
Irrigation, 118, 181
Island alum root, 135
Israel, 22
Italy, 96
Ithuriel's spear, 61
Ivy, 158, 159
Jack-in-the-pulpit, 28
Jade plant, 154
Japan, 72
Japanese gardens, 13
Japanese maples, 62, 63
Juncus, 116
Junipers, 10
Kale, ornamental, 58, 59
Kenya, 95
Kirk, Donald, 31
Kniphofia, 21, 136
Lacewing, 4
Ladies' tresses, 110
Ladybugs/lady beetles, 4, 80, 85
Ladyslipper, 28, 110
Lamb's ears, 11, 77, 148
Lamium, 58
Landscape fabric, 40
Lantana, 11, 88, 153
Larvae, 4
Lateral shoots, 152
Lavandula, 11, 22, 63, 73, 74, 81, 82, 153, 189
Lavatera, 11, 88, 153
Lavender cotton, 136
Lavender, 11, 22, 63, 73, 74, 81 , 82, 153, 189
Lawn clippings, 39
Lawn, 65, 117-120, 132

Layering, 154
Leaching, 48
Leaf mold, 26
Leaf spot, 51
Leaflets, 30
Least toxic method, 4, 80
Least toxic treatments, 173
Lebanon, 22
Leeks, 22, 59
Lemon balm, 73, 74
Lemon basil, 74
Lemon grass, 73
Lemon thyme, 73
Lemon verbena, 73, 74
Lemon, 22
Lentils, 22
Lettuce, 53, 54, 59
Libya, 22
Licorice plant, 77
Ligustrum spp., 11
Lilac, 13
Lilac, California 124, 133, 135
Lilium, 53, 61,112-113
Lily, 53, 59, 61, 112-113, 124, 134
Lily-of-the-Nile, 21
Lin Yun, 13
Linaria, 88
Lippia dulcis, 73
Liriope spp., 11
Lithocarpus densiflora, 10
Lobularia maritima, 5, 189
Locust, black, 158
Lorquin's Admiral, 88
Lovage, 88
Madrone, 144
Magnesium, secondary nutrient, 46, 47
Magnolia, deciduous, 62
Mahonia, 93, 133,134
Maianthemum dilatatum, 145
Mallow, 194
Manganese, micronutrient, 46, 47
Manure, 26
Manzanita, 11, 93, 133
 Maple, 11
Maple, Japanese, 141-142
Marigold, 54, 74, 77, 83, 147, 195
Marin County Stormwater Pollution Prevention Program, 158

~ Index ~

Mariposa lilies, 60
Matricaria recutita, 73
Mayten tree, 21
Maytenus boaria, 21
Mealybugs, 96
Medicinal plants, 161
Mediterranean climate, 20-22, 24, 96, 143
Mediterranean species, 159, 161
Melissa officinalis, 73
Methane, 37
Mexican sage, 3, 13, 23-25, 54, 75
Michaelmas daisy, 88
Microelements, 46
Microscopic organisms, 33, 63
Migration, 89
Mildew, 25, 54, 181
Milkweed, 87. 88
Mimulus, 123, 124, 136
Mineral deficiencies, 51
Mint, 15, 72, 158, 161
Miscanthus sinensis, 116
Mite, fuchsia gall, 107
Mites, predatory, 172-173, 192, 193
Mites, spider, 172-173, 192
Mock orange, 11
Mold, 26, 193
Moles, repelling, 54
Mollusks, 174
Molybdenum, micronutrient, 46, 47
Monarch butterfly, 87, 88
Monkey flower, 88, 123, 124, 136
Monkey puzzle tree, 21
Monte, Ricardo and Sara, 141
Moraea, 148
Morocco, 22
Mowing, 118, 119
Mt. Vision fire, 9
Muir Woods, 26
Mulberry, 13, 153
Mulch, 10, 36-41, 63, 123, 144, 149, 158
Mustard, 196
Myoporum, 11, 70, 158
Myrica californica, 92, 133
Myrrhis odoratat, 73
Myrtle, 22, 133
Myrtus communis, 22
Nandina, 62
Narcissus spp., 22

Nasturtiums, 21, 54, 83
Native plants, 10, 59, 60-61, 90, 92-93, 159
Naturalizing plants and bulbs, 59
Nectar, 85, 87, 163
Neem oil insecticide, 99
Nematodes, 2, 54, 193
Nemophila menziesii, 188
Nepeta faasseni, 136
Nettles, 87, 88
New England asters, 77
Nickel, 46, 196
Niger thistle, 90
Nitrates, 33
Nitrogen, 3, 36, 40, 43, 46-49, 51, 69, 118
Nodes, 153
Novato, 23
Noxious weeds, 10
Nursery, Great Petaluma Desert, 127
Nut hulls, 39
Nutrients, 36, 44, 47, 50
Oak root fungus, 30
Oak, 10, 11, 22, 29, 69, 54, 88, 123, 132-134, 135-137, 138-140, 144
Oakland fire, 9
Oaks, plants for under, 29, 30, 135-137
Ocimum basilicum citriodora, 73
Oenothera hookeri, 86
Oil, horticultural, 171, 173, 182, 183, 184, 192
Oleander, 11
Olives, 22
Onions, 53, 54, 59, 66
Ontario, 97
Oranges, 13, 22
Orchid tree, 13
Orchids, 109-111, 149
Oregano, 81
Oregon grape, 93, 133
Oregon, 98
Organic matter, 33, 34, 35, 36, 42, 46, 47, 48, 49, 51, 58
Oriental poppies, 58
Osteospermun, 21
Oxalis cernua, 160
Oxalis oregana, 144, 160
Oxalis pexcaprae, 160
Pacific Coast Hybrids (PCH) iris, 60
Pacific dogwood, 11
Painted Lady, 88

Palm trees, 54
Pampas grass, 10, 157
Pangue, 21
Pansies, 58
Paphiopedilum, 110, 111
Parasitic wasps, 4
Parrotfeather, 197, 198
Parsley, 86
Passiflora incarnata, 83
Passionflower, 83, 157
Peach, 13
Peanut hulls, 40
Pear, 13
Peas, 53, 59, 66, 151
Peat moss, 26, 35, 38, 63
Pelargonium, 11, 21, 93, 95-98
Pellaea, 30
Pennisetum setaceum 'Rubrum', 15
Penstemon, 11, 15, 58, 134
Pentagramma triangularis, 30
Peperomia, 154
Peppers, 22
Perennials, 53, 58, 64, 77, 147
Permeability of soil, 36
Persimmon, 13
Peruvian lily, 21
Pest control, 166-186
Pest management, 78
Pesticide labels, 183-186
Pesticide, 2, 5, 40, 50, 91, 117, 119, 165, 170, 173, 188, 191
Petunias, 54
Pewee, western wood, 90
pH, 27, 47, 99
Phalaenopsis, 110, 111
Philodendron, 154
Phlox, 58
Phormium, 116
Phosphorus (P) on fertilizer label, 46-49
Phosphorus, 102
Photinia serrulata, 70
Phytophthora, 138-140
Phytoremediation, 196-198
Picea spp., 10
Pickleweed, 197
Pincushion flower, 134
Pine needles, 39, 41
Pines, 10

pinnae, 30, 31
Pinus spp., 10
Pipevine Swallowtail butterfly, 87, 88
Pittosporum, 11, 157
Plaintain, rattlesnake, 110
Platanthera, 110
Platycodons, 13
Plum tree, 62
Podocarpus, 21
Point Reyes, 23
Pollen, 86
Pollination, 164
Pollinators, 86, 90
Pollution, 196-198
Polypodium, 29, 31, 130, 134
Poplar, 153, 196, 198
Poppy, Matilija, 134
Potash/potassium (K) on fertilizer label, 46-49
Potassium (K) on fertilizer label, 46-49
Potassium dihydrogen phosphate (PDP), 182
Potatoes, 53, 54
Potting soil, 78, 152
Powdery mildew, 180
Predator insects, 170, 173
Predators, 176
Primrose, Mexican evening, 158
Privets, 11
Propagation, 99, 147-149, 152-154
Protozoa, 2
Pruning, 4, 27, 55-57, 67-70, 96, 181
Prunus, 92
Pteridium aquilinum, 30
Purple coneflower, 82, 88
Pyracantha, 58
Pyrethrins, 185
Pyrethrum, 120
Pyrophytes, 9
Quail, 86, 92
Queen Anne's Lace, 86, 189
Quercus, 11, 22, 29, 123
Quince, 62
Rabbits, 54
Radishes, 53, 66, 87
Raptors, 90
Rats, 44, 157
Recycle garden waste, 42
Red Admiral, 88
Red hot poker, 21, 136, 148

~ Index ~

Redwood sorrel, 143, 144
Redwood trees, 11, 29, 54, 143-125
Resistance, 4, 96, 99
Rhamnus californica, 92, 133, 145
Rhizome, 60, 128, 129,147
Rhododendron, 15, 47, 63, 145, 154
Ribes, 93, 133
Rice hulls, 39, 63
Rice, 197
Rockrose, 11, 22
Rocks, 13, 14-15
Rockspray, 158
Romney coulteri, 134
Root development, 120
Root pathogens, 49
Rooting hormone, 153, 154
Rose, 54, 62, 67, 68, 86, 93, 133, 153, 180-182, 191-193
Rosehips, 73, 86
Rosemary, 15, 22, 73, 74, 81, 82, 88, 136
Rot, 25
Rudbeckia, 77, 189
Runoff, 48
Rushes, 116
Rust, 51, 180
Sage, 73, 81, 149
Salix spp., 11
Salts, 48
Salvia, 10, 13, 58, 62, 63, 73, 88, 123, 133, 194
Sambucus, 93, 133
Sand, 33, 34
Sandhill sage, 124
Sanseviera, 127, 154
Santa Barbara daisies, 62, 136, 161, 189
Santolina, 11, 63, 134, 136
Sausalito, 23
Saxifragaceae, 98
Scabiosa, 77, 134
Scales, 169-171, 192, 193
Scented geraniums, 21, 64, 95-97
Secondary nutrients, 46
Sedge, 116
Sedum, 11, 15, 88
Seeds of Change, 150
Selenium, 197, 198
Sequoia sempervirens, 11
Sexual reproduction, 152
Shade plants, 26-28

Shoots, lateral, 152
Shoots, terminal, 152
Shrubs, 77
Sidalcea malvaeflora, 88
Silt, 33, 34
Silver spreader, 158
Sisyrinchium, 124
Skippers (butterfly), 88
Slugs, 2, 39, 64, 65, 80, 174-176
Smilacina, 145
Snails, 2, 39, 64, 65, 80, 174-176
Snake plant, 127
Snapdragon, 58, 88, 195
Soap, insecticidal, 171, 173, 183, 192
SOD, 138-140
Soil organisms, 2, 3, 36, 46, 63
Soil, 33-35, 45, 47, 48, 51, 62, 97, 119, 144
Solomon's seal, 28
Sori, 30
Sorrel, redwood, 143, 160
South Africa, 21, 96
South America, 89
Spain, 22, 96
Spartium spp., 10
Spider mites, 96, 172-173
Spiders, 166-168
Spinach, 59
Spiranthes, 110
Spray, hot pepper, 183
Springtails, 2
Spruces, 10
Squash bugs, 54
St. John's wort, 82
Stachys byzantina, 11, 77
Statice, 53, 88
Stevia rebaudiana, 73
Strawberry, 136, 159
Strybing Arboretum, 107
Succulents, 15, 126-128
Suckers, 68
Sudden Oak Death, 138-140
Sulfur, 46, 47, 51, 99, 171, 173,182
Sunburn, 51
Sunflower, 5, 86, 195
Sweet alyssum, 5, 58, 189
Sweet cicely, 73
Sycamore, 153
Syrphid flies, 4

Tagetes, 77
Tamarisk, 158
Tanacetum parthenium, 82
Tanglefoot, 171, 177, 193
Tea gardens, 72-74
Terminal shoots, 152
Terra Nova Nursery, 98
Teucrium, 15
Thatch, 119
Thinning cuts, 56, 67
Thistles, 87
Thrift, common sea, 124
Thyme, 15, 54, 81
Tobacco, tree, 158
Tomatoes, 22, 54
Toxic gases, 38
Toxicity, labels, 185
Toyon, 11, 90, 92, 194
Trace elements, 46
Traps, sticky tape, 171
Tree of heaven, 158
Trillium, 28, 60, 145
Tropaeolum majus, 21, 83
Tulips, 22, 58, 60, 66
Tunisia, 22
Turkey, 22, 96
Turnips, 59
Typha, 116
Umbellifers, 10, 86, 88, 195
University of California Berkeley, 107, 197
Vaccinium ovatum, 145
Valerian, 161
Vancouveria planipetala, 145
Vegetables, 59, 77
Verbena, 88
Viburnum, 62, 153, 194
Vinca spp., 11
Vinegar, wine, 182
Vines, 77
Violets, 28, 83, 144, 154
Viruses, 50
Wake robin, 145
Wandering Jew, 154
Wasp, parasitic, 191
Water, 12, 48, 50, 78, 48
Water sprouts, 56, 69
Webworm, sod, 120
Weeds, 37, 156-158

West Coast Lady, 88
Western Tiger Swallowtail, 88
Wetlands, 197
Wheat, 22
Whitefly, 80, 96
Wild Edible Plants, 31
Wildflowers, 28, 59
Wildwood Farms, 141
Willows, 153
Wisteria, 68, 154
Wood chips, 39
Woodwardia fiimbriata, 130
Worms, 2, 63, 86
Wormwood, 81
Wright, Jerry, 127
Yang, 12
Yarrow, 5, 15, 53, 80, 88, 103, 124, 134, 136, 148, 190, 194, 195
Yin, 12
Zantedeschia aethiopica, 11, 21
Zauschneria californica (Epilobium canum), 11, 86, 134, 160
Zen Buddhism, 72
Zinc, micronutrient, 46, 47
Zinnia, 88, 195